The Hamlyn History
of the World in Colour
Volume Fourteen

AN
AGE OF REVOLUTION

The Hamlyn History
of the World in Colour
Volume Fourteen

AN
AGE OF
REVOLUTION

Advisory Editor
R. R. Palmer
Professor of History,
Yale University

Text by
Esmond Wright
J. J. Tumelty

Paul Hamlyn
London New York Toronto Sydney
PRINTED IN FRANCE — BY BRODARD AND TAUPIN

Based on an original French work
Connaissance de l'Histoire © 1967
Librairie Hachette.
Illustrations © 1967 Librairie Hachette.
English text © 1969 The Hamlyn
Publishing Group Ltd.
SBN 6001 3953 0
First English edition 1969
Phototypeset by Oliver Burridge
Filmsetting Ltd., Crawley, Sussex
Printed in France by Brodard et Taupin,
Paris, for The Hamlyn Publishing Group
Ltd, London, New York, Sydney, Toronto,
The Centre, Feltham, Middlesex, England

Contents

Introduction By R. R. PALMER

All periods are ages of transition, but the fifty years treated in the present volume are the classic Age of Revolution. There is more in revolution than transition of a particularly rapid and violent kind. The reader of this book will find plenty of violence in the form of war, internal struggle and forcible suppression of adversaries, and he will also find a sometimes bewildering story of speedy change. But revolution is more than chaos, and the revolutions in the western world— the Puritan revolution in England, the Russian Revolution, and the American and French Revolutions—have all had a constructive purpose and outcome.

It has been wisely said that a revolution is an unlawful change in the conditions of lawfulness. It begins by defying an older authority and ends by creating a new one. Revolution is always illegal, but its aim is not lawless. Quite properly, therefore, Esmond Wright concludes with the establishment of the new government of the United States, and James Tumelty with the legal codes and other arrangements by which Napoleon organised modern France.

There is good reason to treat the American and the French Revolutions together. It is true that France and the Thirteen Colonies were in many respects very different. France was ten times as populous, more urbanised and more civilised, and much more troubled by the problems of wealth, poverty and privilege with which an old and complex society is often afflicted.

Yet events in the two countries formed part of a larger whole. It was French support that enabled the Americans to win a clear decision in their war of independence. That war, was in fact, one of the series of Anglo-French conflicts that ran intermittently from the time of Louis XIV to that of Napoleon. But in thus helping to dismember the British Empire, the French monarchy was only briefly to enjoy its moment of revenge. The expense of the American war turned its chronic deficits into financial paralysis and brought about a breakdown of the social order. The example of rebellion in America led directly to the French Revolution.

While educated Americans, such as John Adams and Thomas Jefferson read mostly English books, they also shared in that European enlightenment for which French writers were the principal spokesmen. On the other hand, various of the French who became revolutionaries in 1789—Lafayette, Mirabeau, Condorcet, Brissot and Mounier —had long talked, thought or written about the American Revolution and the new American ideas.

The ideas shared in France and America were to inspire all the liberal and democratic movements of modern times. Some had been anticipated in England in the seventeenth century. Some were again expressed in demand for reform in England. Scotland and Ireland, which became audible at about the time of the American Revolution, and made itself increasingly heard until the days of Gladstone.

Similar ideas existed in most other parts of Europe also. It thus happened that when, during the French Revolutionary and Napoleonic wars, the French occupied Italy or Germany, Holland or Poland, they found men in those countries who were willing to work with them. The Revolution 'expanded'. The French empire under Napoleon may have resembled the German control of Europe under Hitler in some ways, but certainly not in spirit. Napoleon appealed to the enlightened and progressive forces in Europe; Hitler loathed them. Hitler annihilated the Jews; Napoleon, while caring nothing for Judaism, insisted that the Jews receive equal rights.

The common fund of revolutionary ideas was mixed, various and internally conflicting. Some ideas fared better than others at different times and in different places, but it is easy to establish a general list. There was the principle of the sovereignty of the people, which sometimes meant national self-determination or independence, and sometimes meant that ultimate authority must lie with the governed and not with the government, a governing class, or a ruling elite or family.

This principle passed into either republicanism or constitutional monarchy. It involved ideas of representation and limited government, which had existed in Europe since the Middle Ages, but now took a more modern form. An equality among citizens, rather than a hierarchy of ranks and orders, was to be the base of representation. Liberty, an old ideal, now carried the ring of individual freedom.

There must be freedom of thought and expression, subject to the needs of public order, which at times, as under Robespierre or Napoleon, were construed to mean the silencing of political opposition. There must be freedom of religion. In the modern state people of any religion or of no religion should enjoy the same civic rights and have the same duties. There should be a written constitution, a document deliberately and rationally contrived and agreed upon, not a mere inheritance of familiar customs and practices.

Closely related was the idea of separation of executive, legislative and judical powers. All magistrates, from the king (if any) downwards, were to possess only a delegated function, and law courts were to be more rational, expeditious and humane. Men had rights, by nature and as citizens, to be specifically declared and secured against arbitrary power. The Americans and the French issued many such pronouncements, and the French Declaration of 1789 was the most memorable document of the era.

But if the French and American Revolutions were alike in some of their ideas, they were also very different. The American was much milder and much less of a revolution. The ruling groups in America before the Revolution were less entrenched, less ostentatiously rich, less obstinate and less detested than in France. British rule was not really oppressive, and before 1776 the British governors and regiments in America were not considered as foreigners. They made themselves very objectionable, but there is a whole school of thought that has seen the American Revolution as a civil war within the British Empire, with discontented persons on both sides of the Atlantic opposing crown and parliament as they then existed. The ultimate cause of the rupture must be found in the fact that England and its colonies had developed in contrary directions in the four or five generations since the first settlement. Relatively speaking, the colonies were already 'democratic', whereas England was in the heyday of its landed aristocracy and the oddities of the unreformed parliament.

The American Revolution is remembered, in part, as the first successful case of colonial independence. It initiated the break-up of the first European overseas empires, and was followed later by the Latin-American revolutions and by increasing autonomy for Canada and the British dominions.

It is sometimes seen also as a precedent for the twentieth-century, anti-colonialist revolutions of Asia and Africa. There are indeed parallels, and the Americans did reject a distant authority that was increasingly felt to be alien. However, the racial feelings and the deeper cultural differences that have animated the recent movements of decolonisation had no part in the American Revolution, especially since at that time it was only the white Americans—then mostly of English or Scottish origin—who counted.

The French Revolution was vaster and more widely significant, and became the prototype of revolution itself. It passed through a series of increasingly radical phases and was opposed by organised counter-revolutionary attempts. It developed a psychology of world liberation, matched by the Austro-Prussian intervention to uphold the French king's authority in 1792. The result was the fall of the French monarchy, more civil struggle, more radicalisation of the Revolution, the Terror, and French military victories that went on interruptedly for twenty years.

In France, unlike America, the whole social structure was transformed. Old forms of income disappeared, such as the right to receive feudal dues and tithes, and also class privileges in taxation which were, in effect, a form of income. Much more real property changed hands, when lands and buildings, both in the towns and in the country, belonging to the Church or to nobles who had fled abroad, were bought up by peasants and the middle classes.

Changes in local government, including a new plan of municipal organisation, altered the social relationships of gentry and common people, and proved more lasting than constitutional reforms at a higher level. The Church was revolutionised from top to bottom. Roman Catholics, Protestants, Jews and the non-religious received the same rights. So did free Negroes. Slavery itself was abolished in the colonies in 1794, although soon restored. Marriage, the family, the schools, and the selection and training of an educated elite were put on a new basis.

The economy was opened up by the abolition of gilds, regional tariffs and older forms of commercial law. It benefited from new technical schools, public museums, the awarding of prizes to inventors, decimal currency and the metric system. War itself was transformed. The army of the citizen soldier, resting on popular enthusiasm and promotion to the highest ranks according to merit (a phenomenon already seen in America but unknown in Europe), was now made more systematic in France, as befitted a country of 25,000,000 inhabitants at war with the powers of Europe.

All such developments heightened the national consciousness, or sense of membership, commitment, unity and common advantage within the state. But the main immediate beneficiaries of the French Revolution were undoubtedly the middle classes, people in town or country who had or could obtain, some property, education and social position. Many of the former aristocracy remained disaffected. The wage-earning and artisan classes received no lasting or tangible satisfaction.

The Revolution was marked by acute class conflict. The beginnings of a working-class movement in 1793 were soon put down. It is true to say that there was in the French Revolution no socialism of any developed kind, but when a revolutionary socialism appeared in the next generation it looked back to the French Revolution for precedent and encouragement. Since the end of the eighteenth century the idea of revolution, either the belief in it or the fear of it, has been a permanent feature of our world.

THE FORMATION OF THE UNITED STATES

	North America	Great Britain	France
1765	Repeal of Stamp Act (1766)	Rockingham becomes prime minister (1765) Earl of Chatham forms government (1766)	Corsica ceded to France (1768) Birth of Napoleon Bonaparte (1769)
1770	Boston 'Massacre' (1770) Boston Tea Party (1773) Quebec Act (1774) First Continental Congress (1774)	Lord North prime minister (1770) Royal Marriages Act (1772) Warren Hastings governor-general of India (1774)	Accession of Louis XVI (1774) Turgot controller-general of finance (1774)
1775	Outbreak of war (1775) Battle of Bunker's Hill (1775) Battle of Trenton (1776) Declaration of Independence (1776) Lafayette in America (1777) Surrender of Burgoyne at Saratoga (1777)	James Cook's third voyage to the Pacific (1776) Death of Earl of Chatham (1778)	Fall of Turgot (1776) Necker director-general of finance (1777) Abolition of serfdom in the royal domains
1780	Surrender of Cornwallis at York-town (1781) Treaty of Versailles: Britain recognises independence of American colonies (1783)	'No Popery' riots in London (1780) Pitt the younger prime minister (1783) Government of India Act (1784)	Dismissal of Necker (1781) Calonne controller-general of finance (1783)
1785	Philadelphia Convention: Establishment of federal government (1787) Franco-U.S. alliance (1788) George Washington first president (1789)	Impeachment of Warren Hastings (1788) Regency crisis (1788)	Affair of the queen's necklace (1785) Dissolution of Assembly of the Notables (1787) Recall of Necker (1788) Summoning of the Estates-General: outbreak of the Revolution (1789)
1790	Creation of a national bank Jefferson founds the Democratic-Republican party (1791) John Adams president (1797) Death of George Washington (1799)	Canada Act (1791) Britain and France at war (1793) Naval mutinies (1797)	Civil Constitution of the Clergy (1790) Abolition of the monarchy (1792) Fall of Robespierre (1794) Formation of the Directory (1795) Establishment of the Consulate (1799)
1800	Washington becomes the capital of the United States	Act of Union with Ireland (1800)	

FAC-SIMILE OF THE ORIGINAL DRAUGHT BY JEFFERSON OF THE
DECLARATION OF INDEPENDENCE
In Congress 4th July, 1776.

The American Revolution

The gap between the Old World and the New; The Continental Congress moves towards self-government; war between Britain and the thirteen colonies; the Declaration of Independence; disaster overtakes the British armies; the brilliant leadership of George Washington; the first successful colonial rebellion; the Founding Fathers establish the groundwork of American democracy.

The beginnings of the conflict

The British colonies in North America in 1763 were not limited to the Atlantic seaboard. They stretched from the Hudson Bay Territory, Newfoundland, Nova Scotia and Quebec in the north, down to the Florida keys in the south and across to the islands of the Caribbean, from Bermuda to Jamaica and from Dominica and St. Vincent to Grenada. Britain also controlled Belize and the Mosquito Coast in Central America. France held the Caribbean sugar islands of Guadeloupe, Saint Domingue (Santo Domingo), Martinique and St. Lucia (which some contemporary observers thought more valuable than empty Canada) and Cayenne in Guiana. Spain held Louisiana, Cuba and Hispaniola. Nevertheless, it was Britain

who dominated both the mainland and the Caribbean with 8,000 ships at sea and 70,000 sailors.

Britain saw its American empire as maritime and its purposes as mercantile. America's raw materials—sugar and rice tobacco and timber, furs and fish—precisely because they could not be produced easily (or at all) at home, were the justification for the colonies' existence. In exchange for all these things the colonies were given military and naval protection and trading bounties, and were sold the manufactures, the cambrics, the necessities and the luxuries which they needed. The British Empire, like all empires, was founded for the profit of the mother country, not its glory. Without this motive, the Empire would not have existed.

The mainland colonies extended for 1,600

miles along the coast of North America, and in 1763 hardly reached more than 100 miles inland. At either end there was a military or naval outpost: Newfoundland was a tiny settlement of 6,000, but its numbers were doubled in the summer as the Grand Banks were swept for cod and mackerel. Florida, won from Spain in 1763, was seen as a frontier against the Spanish-controlled west and against Spain's Indian allies—the Creeks, the Choctaws and the Cherokees. To the acquisitions of 1713—the Hudson

Above: the Declaration of Independence was largely Thomas Jefferson's handiwork, but he was aided by Benjamin Franklin and John Adams. It is celebrated in the United States each 4 July, though not all the names were signed on that day.

The French were fascinated by the American Indians and hoped that, with their aid, they would be able to confine the British settlements to the coastal regions. *Below*: Indians practising with bows and arrows. (*Bibliothèque Nationale, Paris.*)

Bay Territory, Newfoundland and Nova Scotia—there was added in 1763 the vast province of Quebec. Nova Scotia had been given a representative assembly in 1758 and by 1775 its population had reached a total of 20,000. Quebec, however, was French in character, unready yet for any form of representative government, with only nineteen Protestant families living outside Quebec and Montreal.

The British colonies, from Massachusetts to Georgia, varied greatly in character, government and economies. By 1763 the majority were under the direct rule of the Crown, except for Pennsylvania, Delaware and Maryland (owned by private families), and the self-governing provinces of Connecticut and Rhode Island, both of which had elective governors and legislatures. The governors, whether appointed or elected, had considerable vice-regal powers, even though they were in almost all cases now dependent for money on the grants made by the colonial assemblies. Whatever their powers and whatever their dependence on Britain for protection and trade, the colonial assemblies were well-established and had all too frequently discussed the issues of taxation and representation along lines familiar in English history.

The social structure of the mainland colonies was aristocratic. Power in Virginia, in South Carolina and in the Hudson Valley lay with the long established families, and it was rooted in the land. The land owned by the Fairfax family in Virginia ran from the coast to the headwaters of the Potomac. Maine was all but a private holding of Sir William Pepperrell, the conqueror of Louisburg. Much of Georgia was owned by Sir James Wright. Even in Congregationalist New England, seating in church, like the lists of students at Harvard and Yale, went according to property and social class: it was 'property, virtue and intelligence' in that order. From these men of property the colonial councils were recruited. These were 'the friends of government'.

Yet colonial society was not a rigid one. The ease with which property was acquired weakened the sense of class division. George Washington, a protégé of the Fairfaxes, was ill-educated and largely self-made. So were John Macpherson, an enterprising ship-

owner of Philadelphia, Benjamin Franklin, who owed everything to his pen and his printing press, John Hancock, the merchant-smuggler and J. S. Copley, the artist. There was abundant opportunity to make one's way into the gentry.

Below these people were the 'middling sort' of clergy and shopkeepers, teachers and craftsmen, and beneath them, in turn, the large working class, many of whom made their way to North America by serving under contract for a term of years. Among the last group were numerous Germans in Pennsylvania and, particularly in the west and on the frontier, Scots-Irish. The working class, too, included men of enterprise: Matthew Thornton of New Hampshire, who signed the Declaration of Independence; William Buckland, who built Gunston Hall; and Charles Thomson, Secretary of the Continental Congress. 'You may depend upon it' said William Allen, an American clergyman and author, 'that this is one of the best poor men's Country's in the World'.

It was, moreover, a growing country. If it moved west slowly before 1763, it pushed more rapidly in that direction once the French threat was removed. It was increasing fast in numbers: high birth rates and large families were the rule. The average number of children a family was 7·5 and the population doubled each generation. 'An old maid or an old bachelor are as scarce among us and reckoned as ominous as a blazing star,' wrote William Byrd. The population in 1763 was almost 2,000,000, of whom approximately one quarter were German and Scots-Irish, and approximately one-fifth Negro. By 1775 it was 2,500,000. By 1790, at the first census, it was 3,929,214, of whom 757,208 were Negroes.

Top left and right: the Indian war dance which was used to arouse martial spirit and excitement. Note the animal masks which were sometimes worn.
Above: the pioneer settlers were isolated and frequently under attack. Therefore they learned to be adept in their own self-defence and to use guns.
Left and right: Indian chiefs liked to adorn themselves colourfully and specially enjoyed exchanging furs and skins for clothes and trinkets, and dressing up as white men.
(Bibliothèque Nationale, Paris.)

13

The problem of the west

Very few contemporaries in 1763 foresaw or predicted independence for the British colonies. Some French observers did, of course, hope for trouble. 'Colonies are like fruits which cling to the tree only until they ripen' was the view of Turgot, the French statesman and economist. Benjamin Franklin, the most balanced and shrewd of observers, foresaw a world in which the weight of population and of economic power would lie on the American side of the Atlantic, although he did not want it to be a future of separate states. In the 1760s Franklin was an 'Old England man'. So were the vast majority of Americans.

There was no reason why in 1763 independence should have been contemplated. The colonies of mainland North America were English foundations, reflecting Old World values and institutions. The sea was

army. North America still seemed a vulnerable, sharply divided and dependent world.

To meet the Indian threat to the frontier communities and to placate the Indians, in 1763 the British government proclaimed that the land west of the Appallachians was an Indian reserve. In the reserve white settlement was forbidden and Indian traders were to be licensed. This liberal measure was largely the achievement of the Earl of Shelburne as president of the Board of Trade and it was designed not only to reassure the Indians but to guarantee the fur trade. It had the further effect of confining the settlers to the coastal and inland areas and thus it was hoped to discourage not only the westward movement but also the growth of population and thus of colonial manufactures.

What was welcome to the Indians was repugnant to the colonists. Land settlers and frontiersmen saw in the proclamation a

time had therefore come for a new policy. It was thorough and thoughtful as would have been expected from George Grenville, the first lord of the Treasury. Ironically, it was also the first stage on the road to revolution.

The Stamp Act

Grenville planned to station a standing army in America to guard the settlements not only against the Indians but against any resumption of French attack, and considered it fair that the colonists should meet one-third of its cost. He sought also to enforce more strictly the Navigation Acts of 1651 and 1660, which had confined colonial manufactures to British or colonial shipping, and in 1764 passed the Sugar Act, by which the duty on sugar and molasses was reduced in order to make it easier to collect. The laws were to be enforced. To raise revenue to meet part of the costs of defence a Stamp Act was to be passed, imposing a duty on newspapers

their line of communication and their trade was linked profitably to Britain by the mercantile system. Their own land boundaries were moving very slowly inland and were menaced by fierce and unpredictable Indian tribes against whom Britain gave protection. The Iroquois of New York might be friendly but the Creeks, Choctaws and Cherokees were not, and there was an ugly war with the Cherokees in 1759–61. In 1763, angered by the prospect of British rule and still more by the prospect of land grabbing by white settlers, the Ottawas rose under their chief, Pontiac. They were defeated in 1761 by Colonel Henry Bouquet, but not before they had captured every western post except Detroit and Fort Pitt, and had killed about 200 settlers and traders. Moreover, they were defeated once again by British regular soldiers, obligingly paid for by the home government and not by any colonial

barrier to be overturned or to be ignored. It was an obstacle in their path to the good bottom land of the western river valleys and hence to profit. It was, they said, an infringement also of the 'sea to sea' clauses of colonial charters, which permitted steady expansion westward.

Many prominent colonists like George Washington at Mount Vernon or Franklin in London seeking a charter for his land project in the Ohio Valley, resented interference with their plans. (Washington in fact ignored the restrictions altogether.) Moreover, the machinery for regulating Indian trade and the military posts established in the west to check further Indian rebellions imposed a heavy financial burden on Britain. The national debt stood at £133,000,000 in 1763, an increase of £60,000,000 in eight years. The extra cost of colonial defence would be crippling. The

and pamphlets, cards and dice, and legal documents. The Stamp Act was a device used in England since 1694. The taxes to be raised by it were much less severe than those in Britain. Colonial opinion was fully canvassed in advance and the colonial agents (appointees stationed in London) fully consulted, but no alternative plan was put up by them. Indeed, the speed with which some

Above and far left: the Indian culture depended on vast stretches of land over which the buffalo roamed. Since hunting was their way of life, the Indians were skilled horsemen and used bows, arrows and spears for weapons. They hunted buffalo because they needed the meat for food and the skins for clothes and tents.
Left: an Indian chief in war paint.
(Bibliothèque Nationale, Paris.)

distinguished colonial figures, such as George Mercer of Virginia and Jared Ingersoll of Connecticut, accepted the posts of stamp distributors, gave no indication of an approaching crisis.

In fact, colonial opposition was instant and all but uniform. In the Virginia House of Burgesses, Patrick Henry presented a series of resolutions, attacking the act and the king. 'If this be treason', he said, 'make the most of it'. In Boston Sam Adams organised a group which took the name 'Sons of Liberty' with the intention of preventing the sale of stamps by threats of direct action against those using them. Eastern merchants boycotted British goods, and delegates from nine colonies met in City Hall, New York, in the so-called Stamp Act Congress, demanding repeal of the act and issuing a 'Declaration of Rights'. This claimed that since the colonists were not represented in Parliament they could not be taxed by it without their consent.

The fact that the British government expected no resistance to its proposals but met a massive protest is an indication of the gap dividing the Old World from the New. It was partly a matter of the geographical distance: 'Seas roll and months pass between the order and the execution', said Edmund Burke. It was partly—and more fundamentally—a matter of national psychology. The New World was now peopled by many who had no ties of affection or concern with England, and who, when they were English, were Dissenters and Nonconformists, by religion and by situation. A distinct attitude was emerging—sombre, evangelical and hostile to the Church of England in religion, close to nature, self-dependent and socially fluid—that was utterly alien to the status-bound ways of England. Some 3,000 miles of isolation from Europe made real representation impossible. The same 3,000 miles made it not only impossible but, increasingly, unsought.

Many colonies were coming to be in practice independent states, as some perceptive governors like Sir Francis Bernard of Massachusetts and Robert Dinwiddle of Virginia recognised. One of the strands that was gradually being severed was the religious one: there was a mounting fear in the colonies of Anglicanism and of the imposition of religious control from London. As in seventeenth-century England, it was to be but one step from 'no bishop' to 'no king'. Dissenting academics and the small schools which acquired the name of log colleges kept the memories of the Puritan Levellers of 1649 alive. When Grenville passed his Stamp Act he had little notion of the mettle of the colonies. The saddest fact of all was that there were few in Britain who were aware of the extent of the differences between them and the colonists or who sensed that there was in the thirteen rival colonies a nation in process of birth. Those who did know were unconsulted and powerless.

Not for the first or the last time Parliament bent before the storm. It did not accept the principle of 'no taxation without representation', since more than ninety per cent of the home population was as much disfranchised as the Americans. Moreover, without any abrogation of sovereignty— indeed a Declaratory Act was passed asserting that Parliament had complete authority to make laws binding the colonist 'in all cases whatsoever'—the government, now headed by the Marquis of Rockingham, repealed the Stamp Act in February 1766. This was partly due to Franklin's skilful pleading at the bar of the House of Commons, still more to the economic consequences of the boycott. However, the colonists felt that they had won round one

of the struggle, and celebrated with bonfires and the erection in New York of statues to King George III and William Pitt. Neither the mood nor the statues lasted long.

The challenge to authority

The colonists' choice of heroes—Rockingham, John Wilkes and William Pitt—was significant. Grenville, with a lawyer's logic, had thought it both lawful and expedient to tax the colonies. Rockingham, one of the earliest of British party leaders, thought it lawful but not expedient. The Earl of Chatham, as Pitt became in 1766, thought it neither lawful nor expedient. He was, however, a frequent absentee from the government he headed in 1766–1768, as a result of

gout and temperament in equal proportions.

In 1767 his chancellor of the Exchequer, Charles Townshend, sought to honour a rashly-given pledge to reduce the land tax at home by raising an American revenue, not from taxes but from duties on certain imports—tea, glass, paper and paints. He believed it was legitimate for Parliament to impose such trade levies. With the revenue he would pay the salaries of colonial governors and judges and free them thereby from colonial control. To stop smuggling, vice-admiralty courts would be strengthened in power and increased in number.

These measures proved to be as unwelcome as the Stamp Act. In his *Letters of a Pennsylvania Farmer* John Dickinson distinguished between acts intended to raise revenue, which he saw as illegal, and those intended to regulate trade, which he accepted as valid. By this standard Townshend's duties on imports were plainly unconstitutional. At this point, indeed, the colonists began to abandon the distinction between internal and external taxes altogether and to take the primitive but very popular line that all taxes, however imposed, were bad, and that government was best which governed least. The Massachusetts General Court issued a circular letter—the work of Sam Adams, James Otis and Joseph Hawley— appealing to the other colonies for common action asserting that only Americans could tax Americans. Governor Francis Bernard of Massachusetts branded it as seditious,

but seven colonies endorsed it.

When John Hancock's sloop 'Liberty' was seized for smuggling, a riot followed in which the over-efficient customs officials were mobbed and had to take refuge in Castle William on an island in Boston harbour. The Boston garrison was strengthened by two regiments of infantry, the 14th and 29th, in an atmosphere that Thomas Hutchinson, Bernard's successor, described as frankly revolutionary. Reports to Parliament on the Boston situation in 1769 led both houses to resolve that 'wicked and designing men' were responsible, and should be suitably punished.

To Sam Adams in Boston the situation was certainly explosive. By 1770 the movement was no longer led by the merchants of Philadelphia or New York, who were now cautious and not a little frightened of the forces they had unleashed. Effective leadership was now in the hands of the 'Sons of Liberty' in New York and the group organised by Adams and operating from 'The Green Dragon' tavern in Boston. To them the presence of British redcoats—'the lobsterbacks'—was both inflammation and pretext. In New York, in January 1770, soldiers and civilians clashed round a liberty pole. There was bloodshed, but no fatalities, in this episode known as 'The Battle of Golden Hill'. In March in Boston the taunting and snowballing of soldiers, first by schoolboys and then by citizens, led to shots being fired, and five Bostonians, one of them a Negro, Crispus Attucks, were killed. The soldiers were acquitted after a skilful and courageous defence by their counsel, John Adams. However, their presence was proving to be not a safeguard but an irritant and they were more often the victims than the masters of the local situation.

After 1770 the soldiers were carefully confined in Castle William and the British government repealed the Townshend duties except for the penny a pound on tea, retained, like the Declaratory Act, to assert a principle that was increasingly being seen to be only a form of words. Ironically even this decision was taken in cabinet by the casting vote of the new prime minister, Lord North. Had it not been taken there might well have been no need in 1773 to aid the East India Company's tea trade and the history of the world might have been different. However, the colonists had also won the second round of the contest. Once again,

Above: the Boston Massacre in 1770. Stones and snowballs thrown at British sentries ended in shots being fired and five colonists were killed.
Left: after 1776 the American cause became a fashion in Europe. This even included a coiffure de l'indépendance. *(Musée de l' Entente fanco-américaine, Blérancourt.)*

under whatever guise, the government had retreated. Now the cause had martyrs too. For revolutions these are more necessary than issues and easier to identify.

Riot and rebellion

Between the second and third rounds of the contest there came an interlude, a return of prosperity and a reaction against the radicals. The merchants abandoned their boycott, and Sam Adams lost control of the Massachusetts Assembly. Yet this was the period when he worked hardest to keep the cause alive, by writing pamphlets under a host of pseudonyms and by the organisation of the 'Committees of Correspondence'. Governor Thomas Hutchinson described the Boston Committee as composed of 'deacons', 'atheists', and 'blackhearted fellows whom one would not wish to meet in the dark'. However, they began to emerge in each colony and to constitute an unelected but nevertheless representative body of those with grievances, providing a basis for intercolonial action, should the crisis ever come. Although there is no evidence that the colonists had serious grievances, Adams' great achievement was to maintain a feeling of unrest and to produce a machine for action. In 1773 the opportunity came.

The British government, alarmed at the near bankruptcy of the East India Company, allowed it to send tea to America without paying the duty of one shilling a pound, thus making it cheaper than smuggled tea. This certainly would have hit hard at smuggling, and at the profits of those, like John Hancock, who traded in smuggled tea. Thus, the third round of the contest began, oddly enough, with a mass protest against cheaper tea.

In December 1773, three ships carrying cargoes of tea reached Boston. Sam Adams addressed a large crowd, estimated at 7,000, on the evils of drinking cheap and legal tea, and from this meeting a group moved to the docks disguised as Indians. They dropped 342 tea chests to the bottom of the harbour, stoving them in as they did so.

This action was difficult to justify and it was indeed condemned by all responsible colonial opinion, including John Adams and Franklin, and by many merchants. Moreover this time the British Parliament was not prepared to yield. Since 1769 it had been considering an inquiry into Massachusetts. The rendezvous of the navy had already been moved from Halifax to Boston. Half-measures would no longer suffice.

In the spring of 1774 further measures were passed. The port of Boston was closed until the tea was paid for. The Massachusetts charter was annulled, and the governor's council was henceforth appointed by the king. Arrangements were made to quarter troops in occupied as well as empty dwellings. Officers or soldiers accused of crimes were to be sent to Britain for trial.

The Quebec Act was also passed. This was planned beforehand and was not intended as a punitive measure, but it was seen as such in the colonies. It killed all hopes of new colonies in the north-west by transferring to the province of Quebec the lands (and the fur trade) between Ohio and the Mississippi, in which Virginia, Pennsylvania, Connecticut and Massachusetts held interests. Moreover, and even more ominously as the colonists saw it, it gave to this region French civil law and the Roman Catholic religion. The regime provided was centralised, in keeping with customs of the province, and there was to be no jury trial. This was a liberal and intelligent measure, drafts for which had existed since 1763. However, Chatham, Burke, Barré and Fox attacked it as pro-French, autocratic and wicked, and the vehemence of their attacks confirmed colonial suspicions. The timing, as distinct from the merits of the measure, was unfortunate. The colonists now feared the use of arbitrary power and the influence of the Roman Catholic and Anglican Churches.

There were now two firm positions. 'The die is cast' said King George III. 'The colonists must either triumph or submit'. Joseph Reed put it differently in a letter from the first Continental Congress to Lord Dartmouth. 'The people are generally ripe for the execution of any plan the Congress advises, should it be war itself'.

The First Continental Congress

The measures passed in 1774 marked the end of the period of economic and commercial grievance. The issues now were clearly political, and were seen as such in the colonies. Resolutions of sympathy and supplies of food reached Boston. When royal governors dissolved assemblies that were loud in their expression of support for Massachusetts, the members promptly formed themselves into illegal provincial congresses. Indeed, in Virginia the call to the first Continental Congress went out from Hays' Tavern, just across the street from the Williamsburg capitol.

This congress, which met in Carpenter's Hall, Philadelphia, in September 1774, was a gathering of fifty-five diplomats from twelve colonies. Each colony except Georgia was represented. John Adams was greatly stirred by it: 'There is in this Congress a collection of the greatest men upon this Continent in point of abilities, virtues and fortunes. The magnanimity and public spirit which I see here make me blush for the sordid venal herd which I have seen in my own Province . . . .'

Adams was especially impressed by the Virginians, and not least by Washington— 'six feet two, and straight as an Indian'. Though not gifted either in speech or with the pen, Washington looked like a soldier and had experience of the west shared by few. He was still loyal to the king but was a critic of Parliament. He never forgave being refused a colonelcy in the French and Indian

government. Minutemen were formed and in all colonies militia forces came into being. When Washington returned home after the Congress, he was offered the command of seven of the militia companies in Virginia. He put on the buff and the blue of Fairfax County and made it the colours of liberty on two continents. Newspapers now openly discussed independence and, as a contemporary put it: 'Sedition flowed openly from the pulpits'. Colonial governors stored arms, not always discreetly.

When a new Parliament assembled at

Left: a peaceful view of the Hudson River, New York. (Bibliothèque Nationale, Paris.)
Below: the Boston Tea Party. In December 1773, young and excited Americans, led by Samuel Adams, Paul Revere and others disguised themselves as Indians, boarded the Dartmouth *and other ships, and threw the cargoes of tea into Boston Harbour. The British government countered with the 'Intolerable Acts'.*
Below left: this engraving shows the ugliness of the hand-to-hand fighting in the war: the colonists used their sabres to good effect.

War. An alliance of north and south—of radicals and merchants plus planters and 'sultans'—began to emerge.

The First Continental Congress was, nevertheless, evenly divided between radicals and moderates—'one-third Tories, another, Whigs and the rest Mongrels', said Adams. Joseph Galloway's plan for a Grand Council to be chosen by the colonial assemblies headed by a president-general and acting as a kind of third House of Parliament, was rejected, although only by a single vote. John Dickinson wanted to move slowly: action should be taken 'peaceably—prudently—firmly—jointly', or, as he said later, 'procrastination is preservation'. There were, however, other voices. The Declaration of Rights and Grievances demanded 'the rights of Englishmen', the repeal of the measures of 1774 and the dismissal of the king's 'designing and dangerous' ministers. And the 'Resolves' forwarded by Suffolk County, Massachusetts, denied all obligation to obey recent acts of Parliament, described George III as a sovereign 'agreeable to compact' and threatened armed resistance. The Continental Association was formed to bring pressure by boycott on British merchants.

In 1774 British authority in Massachusetts all but collapsed. County conventions and a provincial congress took over the functions of the legally constituted

Westminster in November, it was fortified by an improved trade with Europe and prepared to be—at last—tough. 'The New England governments are in a state of rebellion', said the king. 'Blows must decide'. In February Parliament recognised the fact of rebellion in Massachusetts, and in August acknowledged that this was equally true of all the other colonies. In April, General Thomas Gage, the military governor of Massachusetts, tried to capture Sam Adams and John Hancock and to seize the stores being assembled at Concord. Paul Revere, by trade an engraver and silversmith, by calling a patriot, gave the alarm to a whole countryside. At Lexington, while on

the retreat, the redcoats were sniped at with deadly result from every hedgerow. They lost 200 men and the Americans 93. This now was war.

The Second Continental Congress

It was against this background that the Second Continental Congress met in May 1775. Sixty-five delegates were there, to be joined by five from Georgia in September. John Dickinson's petition, known as the 'Olive Branch' petition, was adopted, only to be scorned in London. In June, Washington was appointed commander-in-chief, and set off to take command of the assembling New England militia outside Cambridge,

Massachusetts. Before his departure he heard of the second open battle of the war, at Bunker Hill, where the British lost 1,150 out of 2,500 engaged. Nevertheless, Washington was appalled at the state of his army and made slow progress in training it and forcing on it a genuine acceptance of rank and discipline.

With Washington in command of an army that was in name opposing not the king but his Parliament, there were now, in a sense, two centres of resistance. Although quite devoid of legality, the Congress acted as the central government, raised troops, established a treasury, issued paper money and negotiated alliances with Indian tribes and European allies. It did so by means of about eighty committees and John Adams was on a great many of them. However, it hesitated about independence. The majority of the population were still opposed to independence. They were still content to claim the rights enjoyed—or deemed to be enjoyed—by British subjects. But, with an army in being, the momentum of events now moved firmly towards separation. John Adams declared that, every day and every post, independence rolled in on Congress like a torrent. Unless Congress acted swiftly, Hawley wrote to Sam Adams, a 'Great Mobb' would march on Philadelphia, purge Congress and set up a dictator.

Britain had declared the colonists to be rebels and proclaimed a blockade. Governor John Dunmore of Virginia called on the slaves to rise in rebellion. British attacks were made or planned against coastal towns like Norfolk and Charleston. Britain was seeking to raise mercenary troops—Germans certainly, and Russians, too, it was rumoured. By May 1776 North Carolina, Virginia and Massachusetts had instructed their delegates in Congress to vote for independence. On June 7th, Richard Henry had introduced his resolution that 'these United Colonies are, and of right ought to be, free and independent States'. Because of the hesitation of Pennsylvania, New Jersey, South Carolina and New York a vote was postponed for three weeks.

Left: a contemporary engraving of George Grenville, who was British prime minister and first lord of the Treasury during 1763–65. He is best remembered for the passing of the Stamp Act (1765), which aroused a storm of opposition among the American colonists. Right: a portrait of the American patriot, John Adams, who first came into prominence through his opposition to the Stamp Act. He was a delegate to the first and second Continental Congresses and later a diplomat. He became president of the United States in 1797 in succession to George Washington.

Above: the advance of the British forces
from Long Island to Manhattan was marked
by many fires.
Left: the wicked British oppressor: a French
caricature. (Musée de l' Entente franco-
américaine, Blérancourt.)
Top right: the siege and capture of Havana
by the British in 1782. (Bibliothèque
Nationale, Paris.)
Bottom right: a portrait of George
Washington. (Musée de l' Entente franco-
américaine, Blérancourt.)

The continental line

It was however the existence of an army that was to prove decisive. The dashing and utterly unreliable Ethan Allen, at the head of his so-called Green Mountain Boys, seized Ticonderoga from a sleepy and incredulous British commander. An expedition to liberate Canada was planned, although it proved a failure. In March 1776, with Washington in control of Dorchester Heights above Boston, the British decided to evacuate the city. When they sailed away they took some 200 loyalist merchants with them. The war was now a civil war also. Behind the formal battles it was a struggle not only between the Old World and the New but over who should rule at home.

The army in the field was the arm of the civil Congress. In July 1775 the Congress had issued its 'Declaration of Causes of Taking Up Arms'. Americans it said, would die rather than be enslaved, but the declaration also stated that independence was not the goal. By July 1776 the hesitations were gone. Washington was partly won over, in January 1776, by reading Tom Paine's pamphlet *Common Sense*. To Paine, who urged an immediate declaration of independence, the king was no God above the battle but 'the royal brute'. The pamphlet sold well. The note of republicanism was struck late, but it became the dominant theme. In the eyes of the colonists it was no longer Parliament that was the tyrant but the king.

Independence

The aims now were separation and republicanism. Congress no longer claimed 'the rights of Englishmen' but 'natural rights'. When Thomas Jefferson, at the behest of Congress, drafted the Declaration of Independence, he claimed that thus far the American people had voluntarily associated themselves with Britain and had voluntarily acknowledged the same king. This king, by his despotic acts (twenty-seven specific charges were listed), had forfeited this allegiance. There was no reference at all to acts of trade or to Parliament. This statement was prefaced by one of the noblest testaments of faith in liberty and in man's capacity for it which has ever been written. 'We hold these truths to be self-evident,

that all men are created equal; that they are endowed by their creator with certain unalienable rights; that among these are life, liberty and the pursuit of happiness. That, to secure these rights, governments are instituted among men, deriving their just powers from the consent of the governed; that, whenever any form of government becomes destructive of these ends, it is the right of the people to alter or to abolish it, to institute new government, laying its foundations on such principles, organising its powers in such form, as to them shall seem most likely to effect their safety and happiness'.

The same sentiments, without the same eloquence but with greater vivacity were expressed by an old soldier to whom John Adams talked many years later.

'"Captain Preston, why did you go to the Concord fight, the nineteenth of April 1775?" The old man, bowed beneath the weight of years, raised himself, and turning to me, said: "Why did I go?" "Yes", I replied. "My histories tell me that you men of the Revolution took up arms against 'intolerable oppressions'". "What were they?" "Oppression. I didn't feel them." "What, were you not oppressed by the Stamp Act?" "I never saw one of those stamps, and always understood that Governor Bernard put them all in Castle William. I am certain I never paid a penny for one of them". "Well, what about the tea tax?" "Tea tax! I never drank a drop of the stuff— the boys threw it all overboard". "Then I suppose you had been reading Harrington or Sydney or Locke about the eternal principles of liberty". Never heard of 'em. We read only the Bible, the Catechism, Wells'

Psalms and Hymns and the Almanack". "Well, then, what was the matter, and what did you mean in going to the fight?" "Young man, what we meant in going for those redcoats was this: we always had governed ourselves, and we always meant to. They didn't mean we should".'

These two views have, in their different ways, become the spirit of the Revolution. The American Revolution was the first successful act of rebellion by a new nation in modern history. The shots fired at Lexington Green and Concord bridge have echoed round the world. Almost all the independent states of Africa and Asia today, and many of the new nations in Europe, would as part of the legend of their own independence find links with 1776. The statues that are grouped outside the White House in Washington are a reminder of those from other nations who then saw in the struggle for American independence a symbol and a portent of the struggle of other nations to be free. It is indeed impossible to calculate the

consequences for the world that have followed from the events that took place on the narrow Atlantic seaboard in the years from 1763 to 1776.

The War of Independence and the constitution

The Declaration of Independence was proclaimed on July 4th 1776. The day before, Sir William Howe seized Staten Island and led a British army ashore from the largest armada which had ever assembled in North American waters. New York was a loyalist centre, and it seemed possible to move up the Hudson Valley from New York to cut off rebellious New England from the other, less resolute colonies and to command the overland route to Canada.

The task of suppressing the rebellion, however distasteful, did not appear to be too difficult. The British had overwhelmingly superior numbers, outmatching the colonies by four to one in manpower and in ships of

cenaries and had a professional army and navy—even if a few of its senior officers like Lord Amherst and Admiral Keppel refused to serve against Americans. Against them were untrained, ill-clad, undisciplined and usually unpaid, militia, led by officers who, with the exception of Charles Lee, Horatio Gates and Washington, had as little experience of war as themselves, and little taste for it.

However, from the first it was for Britain a story of tactical successes left unexploited, of basic strategic errors and of some irredeemable disasters. Sir William Howe put his men ashore on Long Island with ease, defeated Washington's army and forced it to retreat across the Sound to Manhattan. He drove up the island with the same unhurried effortlessness and Washing-

ton made another hasty retreat over the Hudson and through New Jersey. The Americans lacked flour, clothing and money to pay their soldiers. Paine wrote in *The Crisis*: 'These are the times that try men's souls. The summer soldier and the sunshine patriot will, in this crisis, shrink from the service of their country; but he that stands it *now* deserves the love and thanks of man and woman'. Washington's view was more laconic: 'I think the game is pretty near up'.

At any of these points Howe could, it seemed, have destroyed the enemy army completely and captured its leader. That he failed to do so was due overwhelmingly to the fact that he saw himself as an arbitrator and diplomat rather than as a soldier. If he pressed them a little more, they would surrender. The diplomat's role did not

war by a hundred to one. Command of the sea—until the entry of the French—allowed them to strike at points of their own choosing. At times, trying to anticipate where the blow would fall, Washington found himself 'compelled to wander about the country like the Arabs in search of corn'. Britain had superior credit, could hire foreign mer-

Left: William Pitt, afterwards Earl of Chatham. He strongly opposed attempts to tax the American colonists and favoured conciliatory moves. From a contemporary portrait.
Above: Alexander Hamilton, a lawyer who played an important part in the drafting of the constitution of the United States. From a portrait.
Right: King George III. He incurred great unpopularity with the American colonists and the colonial policies he adopted were largely responsible for the outbreak of the American Revolution. From a portrait.

harmonise with the soldier's. After each tactical triumph he expected negotiations to begin. On the other hand, British morale was being steadily eroded by the procrastination and delays.

On Christmas night, 1776, Washington carried through one of his cleverest manoeuvres of the war, and certainly the most psychologically effective. He crossed the Delaware with 2,400 men, surprised Colonel Rall and his still festive German troops at Trenton, and took 1,000 prisoners. Colonel Rall paid for his card game with his life. Leaving his campfires burning to deceive the hurriedly summoned British reserves, Washington outflanked them and appeared at Princeton to strike again. By the time both armies went into winter quarters—war was still a game played according to a gentlemanly calendar—Howe's troops were no longer safe beyond the Hudson, and Washington had regained the advantage. If he failed to stop the transfer of Howe's forces in 1777 to Philadelphia, he at least managed to hold his own small force together.

The road to Saratoga

The winter of 1777–78 was the real testing time—one that tried not only men's souls but their stomachs. Valley Forge, where the American troops were quartered, was, said Washington, 'a dreary kind of place and uncomfortably provided'. 'Poor food—hard lodging—cold weather—fatigue—nasty clothes—nasty cookery—vomit half my time—smoked out of my senses—the devil's in't—I can't endure it', wrote Surgeon Albigence Waldo. But the Americans did endure. They were now better drilled than ever before thanks to Friedrich Von Steuben, the Prussian soldier who had offered his services to Washington. Washington's greatest achievement was to keep an army in being at Valley Forge. He said afterwards that Howe could still have won the war had he attacked at that point. By October 1777, however, it was beginning to look too late for a British victory.

While Howe was taking Philadelphia and relaxing in its comfort, General John Burgoyne, with 7,000 men and a vast baggage train, was seeking to cut a path south from Canada via Lake Champlain and the Hudson Valley. The intention was to bring reinforcements to Howe (who, Burgoyne had expected, would come north to meet him), to cut off New England permanently and to divert Washington's attention.

However, Burgoyne's transport was inadequate. One of his raiding columns hunting for food in Vermont was destroyed

Left: Lord Rockingham (right) and Edmund Burke. Burke was secretary to Rockingham when the latter became prime minister in 1765 and defended Rockingham's repeal of the Stamp Act in Parliament. Both men sought reconciliation with the American colonists.
Above: 'The world turned upside down'. The British surrender at Yorktown, October 1781 (Musée de Versailles.)
Below: an engraving of George Washington's home on the Potomac River. (Bibliothèque Nationale, Paris.)

by the Green Mountain Boys. A parallel force, which was to move down the Mohawk River to join him, gave up the attempt and went back to Canada. Meanwhile, the American force under Horatio Gates that blocked his path increased in numbers and in spirit day by day. By the end of September Burgoyne was outnumbered four to one. On 14th October he surrendered at Saratoga, abandoning arms and supplies, and undertaking that his men would not serve any further against the Americans. This was not only a British disaster, it was a humiliation and it proved to be the turning point in the war.

France intervenes

Until the news of Saratoga the French had hesitated about giving open support to the Revolution. The French monarchy had no taste for governments that were overthrowing kings. However, any dissension in Britain's colonies was worth cultivating. On the outbreak of war, Congress sent to Paris a three-man team to act as negotiators for money, supplies and (hopefully) for an open alliance with France. The quest for foreign aid had been active from the start. The new nation wanted the commercial contracts with Europe which the colonial mercantile system had banned. And it not only sought them in themselves. Without foreign aid it could not long survive.

The three men who served as emissaries were the irascible and self-important Arthur Lee from Virginia, the wily merchant-politician Silas Deane from Connecticut (who proved to be in Britain's pay and passed everything on to the British government) and Benjamin Franklin, who became the principal agent and ambassador. During his years in Paris (1776–85), when he was already over 70, Franklin emerged not only as the architect of the alliance but as the favourite of the *salons* of Paris, admired and worshipped as both scientist and diplomat, man of affairs (both business and amatory) and, indeed, as Jean-Jacques Rousseau's 'natural man' made visible. There were Franklin rings, Franklin snuff boxes and even Franklin chamber pots. His wig, worn to hide his eczema, became a symbol of liberty. The old man was amused, and he not only enjoyed the experience but exploited it.

From the first the French were prompt

with aid, 1,000,000 livres being given through the fictitious company, Rodrigue Hortalez et Compagnie. Spain proved equally generous. However, aid could not be openly avowed without inducing a declaration of war by Britain. The surrender of Saratoga led to the planning of a peace mission by Britain, and Franklin craftily allowed it to be known in Paris that he favoured its prospects. France moved towards open intervention and in February 1778 the Treaty of Alliance was signed—the United States' first entangling alliance. France recognised the United States as independent and each country undertook not to make a separate peace. Each also undertook to treat the other commercially as a 'most favoured nation'.

Spain entered the war a year later not as an ally of the United States but as an ally of France. Its motive was the reconquering of Gibraltar, which the Spanish besieged for four long years. By 1780 Britain was also at war with Holland and with the League of Armed Neutrality (Denmark, Sweden, Portugal and Russia). The war was now a world war. It was fought in places as far apart as India and the Caribbean. The American naval commander, John Paul Jones, provisioned from Brest, raided the Scottish and Yorkshire coasts, and a French landing in Ireland was planned. The American theatre of war now became in British eyes little more than a side-show.

The road to Yorktown

This dramatic transformation of the situation was a great relief for the Americans. French aid was in any event substantial. French gifts and loans amounted in the end to $8,000,000, a large sum for an eighteenth-century war. The entry of France also helped to guarantee the Dutch loans to the United States. With money there also came men and ships. After 1778 French fleets prowled the Atlantic coast, and Britain lost its naval preponderance. The operations of the French naval commander, the Comte d' Estaing, diverted British troops to the West Indies and speeded the evacuation of Philadelphia in 1778 and Newport in 1779. It was the appearance of a French fleet off the Virginian coast that sealed the fate of a British army under Lord Cornwallis at Yorktown in 1781. The siege of Yorktown itself was made possible by the presence alongside Washington's army of 9,000 regular French troops commanded by the Comte de Rochambeau, and with the Marquis de Lafayette, one of the earliest and most fanatical of French volunteers, leading a brigade. When General O'Hara, deputising for Cornwallis—who feigned illness—surrendered his sword, he sought to surrender it to Rochambeau. Rochambeau refused and indicated Washington. Lafayette, for his part, never forgot his American experience and at the beginning

of the French Revolution saw himself as playing a Washington. If his role in French history never in fact matched his own hopes for it, the French Revolution certainly owed much to the enthusiasm of those who had helped the American cause.

The Treaty of Paris

With the surrender of Cornwallis at Yorktown, the war was virtually over. King George III was with difficulty dissuaded from abdicating. Lord North resigned as prime minister in March 1782, Shelburne becoming first secretary of state and, on

Above right: the Marquis de Lafayette was one of the first of many Frenchmen who fought for the American cause. He saw it not only as a great adventure but also as an international crusade. 'The welfare of America', he said, 'is ultimately bound up with that of mankind'. (Musée de Versailles.)
Centre: caricature of Edmund Burke who also saw the American cause as the cause of liberty. 'A great empire and little minds', he declared, 'go ill together.' (Musée de l' Entente franco-américaine, Blérancourt.)
Above left and opposite: war is more boredom than battle and in the camps of the French troops relief and escape took many forms. (Musée de l' Entente franco-américaine, Blérancourt.)

Below: from the outset of hostilities between the British and Americans, France had secretly aided the Americans with supplies and the picture shows ships being loaded at Brest. (Musée de la Marine, Paris.)
Left: volunteers were also secretly recruited in support of the American cause.

Rockingham's death, prime minister. At first Shelburne opposed the idea of independence but not for long. With the merchant Richard Oswald as his emissary in Paris, negotiations were opened with Franklin in April 1782 and concluded in November of that year. Franklin broke his word in concluding a separate peace, but in the thick air of spying and counter-spying in Paris it was hardly possible for the French foreign minister, Vergennes, to be unaware of what was happening.

By the terms of the treaty Britain recognised the independence of the United States and accepted its western boundary as the Mississippi River. Britain conceded the right of navigation on the Mississippi and fishing rights off Newfoundland. Congress agreed to recommend to the individual states that they indemnify the loyalists and pay their debts to Britain. This was easy to say but hard to implement.

The United States won more by diplomacy than its victories entitled. If Saratoga and Yorktown were disasters for the British, this was in large measure due to their own folly. By 1783, however, Britain had averted direct invasion, and Admiral Rodney's victory in 1782 off Dominica in the West Indies gave Britain additional bargaining power. Spain and France had not done particularly well out of the war. Spain regained the Floridas, for whatever value they might be, but not Gibraltar. France won some West Indian islands and a huge debt, the full interest on which would be six years in

falling due. For the Americans, who had caused the war, it was a total triumph.

The critical period

Yet by 1783 the evidence of triumph was hard to see. The new nation had not acquired a written constitution until 1781, the 'Articles of Confederation', drafted by John Dickinson. These provided for a single-chamber government in which each state had one vote. There was no president and no supreme court. The government was in form and in fact a federal union of unwilling members. Congress had no power to levy taxes, regulate commerce, raise an army or enforce the laws. In the last years of the war Congress had even been driven from Philadelphia when unpaid regiments rebelled.

There was no power to enforce even the Treaty of Peace. Moreover, Congress could not enforce uniform import duties against foreign countries or prevent the customs and boundary wars of state versus state. For money it relied on issues of paper, which depreciated fast—'not worth a Continental' is still a phrase in use in the United States. Some states printed their own paper money and other states refused to honour it. When in Massachusetts creditors foreclosed on the properties of the debt-ridden farmers, about 1,500 of them, led by Daniel Shays, seized the arsenal at Springfield and closed the courts.

The economic situation was worsened by the exclusion of the new state from the

British Empire and the loss of trade with the West Indies. British markets, bounties and guarantees were also lost. Britain retained the fur posts, claiming that loyalists had not been indemnified or debts to British merchants repaid. There was no matching power of retaliation available to Congress.

This period, from 1781 to 1787, was given the name of 'The Critical Period' by the American historian, John Fiske, in 1888, and he attributed the difficulties to the lack of real sovereignty in the existing government, that is, the government under the articles of confederation, agreed on by 1781. The commercial crisis, however, was due not to the Articles but to the end of the wartime boom and to the dislocation of American trade that followed it. Congress could have done little to affect this. Moreover, no direction by it to the states to honour their debt or to treat the loyalists sympathetically would have had much influence, when there was no general wish to do either.

However, the diplomatic achievements of the period were considerable. The Treaty of Paris and the North-West Ordinances of 1785 and 1787, were remarkable by any standards. The first of the Ordinances provided for a system of land surveys based on townships six miles square and subdivided into thirty-six sections. The latter set out the stages whereby a territory (5,000 inhabitants) and finally a state (60,000 inhabitants) would be established. Out of the entire territory of the old north-west five states

Above and left: in 1778 France made an open alliance with the United States and after the signing of the treaty an expeditionary force was formed. (Musée de l' Entente franco-américaine, Blérancourt.)

were in the end formed: Ohio, Indiana, Illinois, Michigan and Wisconsin. In them freedom of religion, trial by jury and due process of law were guaranteed, slavery was forbidden and the newly-created states were seen and treated as equal in importance to the original thirteen. The west was peopled fast. This generous and farsighted provision, essentially the handiwork of Thomas Jefferson, was to prove almost as significant as the constitution itself. It was its federal character as much as its republican constitution that made the United States in the nineteenth century the 'last best hope of man'.

The constitution

Nevertheless the political weaknesses of the Articles pointed to a need for revision. James Madison of Virginia persuaded his state to discuss with Maryland their common interest in the navigation of Chesapeake Bay and the Potomac. The Mount Vernon Conference in 1785 established the need for a wider agreement and all the states were invited to Annapolis in 1786 to discuss interstate commercial regulations. Five states sent representatives—New York, New Jersey, Virginia, Pennsylvania and Delaware.

Alexander Hamilton, the brilliant young West Indian-born lawyer, who had served as Washington's aide-de-camp, moved a resolution to invite all the states to meet the following year to revise the Articles. Fifty-five men, representing all the states except Rhode Island, met in the Philadelphia State House in May 1787. They decided on a totally new document and they hammered out agreement on it through the long, hot summer. They ended by drawing up a constitution, 4,000 words in length, for a farmer's republic of 3,500,000 people. The same document, amended only occasionally and mainly in inessentials, is still the binding form of government for a vast cosmopolitan society of more than 200,000,000 people living across and beyond a continent. The Founding Fathers were remarkable men. Thomas Jefferson called them an assembly

The second major compromise appeared at this time as less important but was to have far-reaching consequences: how were slaves to be counted both for representation and for taxation? The northern states, with businessmen's logic, wanted slaves excluded from representation, since they were neither citizens nor voters, but included for tax purposes, since they were property. In other words, they themselves had few slaves, and they wanted it both ways. The south disagreed: it did not want to be taxed without

of demi-gods.

There was much on which the delegates agreed: a written constitution, the separation of powers, the need for the federal government to be strong and have the power to declare war and make peace, and to tax and regulate commerce. There was much on which agreement was reached only slowly by careful compromise. Perhaps the most serious basic political disagreement was on the issue of representation. The large states, whose case was presented by Edmund Randolph of Virginia, favoured a bicameral legislature, with representation in each based on size of population. There was also to be a single executive and judiciary, both chosen by the legislature. This caused bitter feeling, for the disparity of the states in size was striking. Delaware had 60,000 people and Rhode Island 68,000. On the other hand, Virginia, which then included Kentucky, had 750,000, of whom 300,000 were slaves. Massachusetts, excluding Maine, had 380,000, very few of whom were slaves.

New Jersey countered the Virginia plan

with its own, presented by William Paterson: a legislature of one house, elected by the states regardless of population, and with an executive consisting of more than one man elected by Congress. After a month's debate agreement was reached on a compromise— the 'Connecticut compromise'—providing for equal representation of each state in the Senate, while maintaining the principle of representation by population in the House of Representatives.

This system is still in force, although, until the 17th Amendment of 1913, the Senate was elected indirectly by the state legislatures and not directly by the people. Yet fears of rivalry between great and small states proved largely illusory. Maryland, a small state, and Virginia, a large one, shared on the Chesapeake a common economy of tobacco plantations and slave labour. Connecticut and Massachusetts had similar commercial interests. The rivalry of state against state has never been as important in American history as the clash of sectional interests.

The American War had a considerable impact on France, and two men made reputations during the course of the war.
Above right: the Comte d' Estaing whose fleet dominated the seas in 1778 and 1779. It was this command of the sea that compelled the Marquis of Cornwallis to surrender at Yorktown in 1781. (Musée de l' Entente franco-américaine, Blérancourt.)
Below left: the Comte de Rochambeau, commander of the French land forces from 1780, and joint commander with George Washington at Yorktown. (Musée de Versailles.)
Far left: with French intervention the war became world-wide and the Caribbean important to both sides. This picture shows the Battle of Martinique between the French and English. (Musée de la Marine, Paris.)
Centre: heroes returned with tales to tell and received a welcome from their parents and fiancées. (Musée de l' Entente franco-américaine, Blérancourt.)

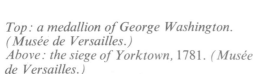

Top: a medallion of George Washington.
(Musée de Versailles.)
Above: the siege of Yorktown, 1781. (Musée
de Versailles.)
Right: when the Marquis of Cornwallis
surrendered Yorktown, he sent General
O'Hara as his deputy to carry out the task.
O'Hara offered his sword to the Comte de
Rochambeau, who refused to accept it and
indicated that it should be surrendered to
George Washington. (Musée de l'Entente
franco-américaine, Blérancourt.)

35

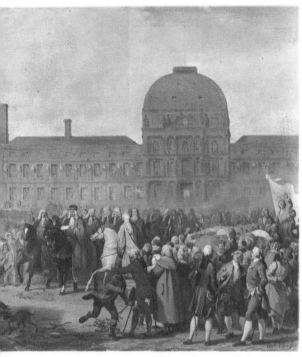

some matching representation. In the end the 'three-fifths' compromise was reached. A slave was counted as three-fifths of a person for purposes of both taxation and representation. It was also agreed that there would be no interference with the importation of slaves until 1808. Slavery was not yet the emotional issue it was to become. Even the revolutionary fires of the French Revolution that led to Toussaint l'Ouverture's rebellion in Santo Domingo sparked few fires in the United States. The most bitter attack at the constitutional convention came in fact from Virginia. As masters on their deathbeds often freed their slaves, as did Washington, slavery was expected gradually to die out.

There was one other basic compromise: on the election of the executive. There were many among the Founding Fathers who distrusted 'the people' and opposed direct election. It was therefore agreed, in the closing stages of the convention, that the president and vice-president should be chosen by an electoral college, equal in number to the number of senators and representatives, meeting in each of the states and forwarding the names of its choice to the federal government. The college still survives, weakened by the growth of political parties, as a curious relic of eighteenth-century political mechanics. It makes it possible for a president to be elected who (as in 1888) has fewer popular votes than his opponent. Furthermore, since a president must have an absolute majority of electoral college votes and not merely be head of the list, it is possible for the choice of president to be thrown to the House of Representatives, voting by states, as was done in 1824. The system is a reminder that, although the three branches of government were nicely balanced by the compromises of 1787, only one half of one branch, the legislature, was directly elected. The president chose the judges, and he himself was indirectly elected.

In all the states there was also a property qualification for the suffrage. As a result it has sometimes been said that the Founding Fathers feared democracy rather than favoured it. Certainly, there were those among them, like Alexander Hamilton and Gouverneur Morris, who thought the constitution a 'weak and worthless' document. Nevertheless, Hamilton himself rendered immense service by the campaign he waged in New York to secure the ratification of the constitution in the New York state convention, and also by writing, with John Jay and James Madison, the series of masterly articles in its support known collectively as *The Federalist Papers*.

It is true that the majority of the delegates at Philadelphia were beneficiaries of the Constitution—investors, land speculators, merchants and slave owners. Moreover, the document was not submitted directly to the people and contained no bill of rights.

Indeed, to meet this criticism a bill of rights was added to it, in the shape of the first ten amendments, ratified in 1791. In other words, the constitution was not perfect, like any other product of the hand of men and a bitter civil war was to be fought in 1861 over the interpretation of it. Yet it was a remarkable document. Its ambiguity, as James Madison, the fourth president of the United States, said, was the price of unanimity. The Founding Fathers knew that paper constitutions would only survive if they were brought to life and made workable by men and women. The American nation has been built up in 1787 and since, not by federal or judicial enactments but by the common life lived and chosen by its members.

Much of the anxiety that the convention might have aroused was removed by the general awareness that, whatever the form

Below: in Paris Benjamin Franklin became a figure of legend, the natural man, 'the good Quaker', 'le Bonhomme Richard'. He was one of the first great political propagandists in modern history, who sold the cause abroad and, in the process, sold himself with great success, much amusement and total cynicism. (Musée de Versailles.)
Top left: the cession of Louisiana by Napoleon to the United States at New Orleans in 1803. (Musée de l' Entente franco-américaine, Blérancourt.)
Bottom left: Paris celebrating the news of the Treaty of Paris in 1783. (Musée de Versailles.)
Bottom far left: this allegory vividly portrays the closeness of the ties between France and the United States and the French view of their own contribution to American independence. (Musée de l' Entente franco-américaine, Blérancourt.)

In 1800 *a commercial convention between France and the United States was signed and celebrated, but this only came about after a period of discord between the two nations. Left: the ratifying of the convention. (Musée de l' Entente franco-américaine, Blérancourt.)*
Below, left and right: life was harsh on the sugar plantations in Santo Domingo and in 1791 the Negro slaves revolted. They were led by Toussaint L'Ouverture, a near illiterate, but nevertheless a man of considerable ability who was able to match some of Napoleon's best generals. In battle he killed more French and British soldiers than either Napoleon or Wellington lost in the Peninsular War. However, he was a just and humane man and a hero to many . . liberals, including the poet Wordsworth. He was captured by the French, imprisoned in the grim Fort de Joux, and died there in 1803. (Bibliothèque Nationale, Paris.)

le Clerc f.

of election, George Washington was likely to be the universal choice for president. With John Adams as his vice-president, Washington took his oath of office on the balcony of Federal Hall, New York, in April 1789. He chose Jefferson (who had succeeded Franklin as U.S. ambassador in Paris) as his secretary of state, Hamilton as secretary of the treasury and Henry Knox (a Massachusetts bookseller turned general), as his secretary of war.

Washington's contribution to the presidency was immense, since all the decisions he took set precedents. He brought dignity and decorum to the office: a coach and four, weekly levees and an address to Congress similar to the British sovereign's speech from the throne. Both the Senate and Supreme Court, he discovered, refused to grant advice before negotiation of treaties or legal cases, so presidential initiative was increased and presidential authority heightened. The judiciary was organised, with a chief justice and five associate justices. Washington's administration was also distinguished by the work of his two brilliant secretaries, Hamilton and Jefferson.

Hamilton believed that the new federal government would be strong only if its credit was thoroughly established. Nations —like individuals—must pay their debts. He therefore recommended to Congress that the national debt, both foreign ($12,000,000) and domestic ($42,000,000), should be paid at face value, and that the federal government should accept and meet the debts contracted by the states. He proposed to do this by funding the debt, that is, by offering a new loan. There was no opposition to the payment of the foreign debt but much to the payment of the domestic one, since speculators (mainly northerners) had been buying up government bonds at cut rates and thus stood to gain appreciably. Moreover, those states like Virginia, which had already begun to meet their obligations, objected to the indirect aid being given to their less generous or less wealthy rivals. However, Hamilton had his way, in part by agreeing to placate the south by locating the planned national capital (then spoken of as the 'federal city') on the banks of the Potomac and near Mount Vernon. This device by Hamilton won the support of the moneyed class for the constitution and the federal government.

Hamilton also set up a national bank, although with Jefferson and Madison opposing what they saw as a monopoly and a threat to the state banks. He also proposed an excise tax and a higher tariff to encourage manufactures, and again he had his way.

Hamilton and Jefferson

Policy-making was one thing; implementation was another. Hamilton's excise tax ran into difficulties. He had urged an excise tax on distilled liquors in part to impress upon the western frontiersmen the powers of the federal government. These men had for a long time been accustomed to convert their corn and rye into whisky, since in this form it was easier to transport over the mountains and more readily saleable. They resented the tax bitterly and in 1794 in Western Pennsylvania they offered resistance to the federal collectors, in what was known as the 'Whisky Rebellion'. Hamilton called out

Above: Thomas Jefferson, third president of the United States, principal author of the Declaration of Independence, ambassador to France after Benjamin Franklin, and founder of the Democratic party. He admired the intentions of the early French Revolutionaries but lost his enthusiasm as the Terror grew. (Bibliothèque Nationale, Paris.)

the militia and, at the display of force, opposition melted away. Hamilton never lost the reputation of having engineered this deliberately and he showed a disposition throughout his career to be over-assertive in government.

Gradually a division on both political and personal matters appeared between Jefferson and Hamilton. The latter was a supporter of strong federal government, of manufacturers, of 'the rich, the well-born and the able,' and of the British connection, and the former an advocate of states rights, freedom for the farmer and support for France. Jefferson began his period in office as an admirer of France and as a sympathiser with the French Revolution. He cooled in these views, partly because of the undiplomatic exuberance shown by the French ambassador, Edmond Genêt.

In 1793, misreading the American scene and invoking the alliance of 1778, he assumed U.S. support for revolutionary France, equipped 'revolutionary' ships to raid British shipping and planned 'liberating' armies that were to march into the Spanish-owned west. In April 1793 Washington issued his neutrality proclamation. In August the cabinet voted to ask the French government to recall Genêt.

Robespierre retorted by asking in return for the recall of Gouverneur Morris, the Arch-Tory minister of the United States to France. In the end Genêt persuaded the U.S. government not to send him back and wisely settled in the Hudson Valley.

Foreign policy divided the two emerging parties as much as economic issues. Broadly, Jefferson and the Republicans were pro-French and the Hamiltonians pro-British. Paradoxically, however, New England and the seaboard towns, normally anti-British because of their trading rivalry, were now pro-British, fearing revolution, French privateering and 'popery'. The Virginian planters, usually pro-British, were now pro-French, because of their taste for Parisian ways and a dislike of Yankee capitalism and Hamilton's excise taxes. From now on the rivalry of parties covered a more fundamental division between sectional interests.

When war between France and Britain began in 1793, inevitably American neutrality was threatened. Britain was still in occupation of the fur posts and proposed to continue to occupy them until the debts left unpaid in 1783 were settled. Britain began to seize U.S. shipping engaged in trade with the French West Indies and to impress U.S. sailors into British service. Although pro-French feeling in the United States declined after Genêt's excesses were revealed (Jefferson himself resigned office in December 1793), nevertheless, Washington was alarmed at the prospect of war with Britain in alliance with a terrorist revolutionary regime in Paris. He was still more worried at the rising tide of war feeling: militia were drilling on village greens and harbours were being fortified.

Accordingly, in 1794 Washington sent Chief Justice John Jay to London to try to settle his disputes with Britain. Jay succeeded in averting war but only at the expense of American national pride. The Jay treaty secured a British promise to evacuate the north-west posts and to submit the boundary and debts question to commissions. However, the United States had to surrender its position on neutral rights. It was given a few concessions in the British West Indies and agreed to open its own ports without restrictions to British shipping. The treaty was as a result extremely unpopular. Jay was burned in effigy, Hamilton stoned in the streets and Washington began now to feel biting public criticism for the first time.

The treaty was in the long run a step towards the use of arbitration in the settlement of disputes. It stimulated the settling of disagreements with Spain and the 1795 Treaty of San Lorenzo allowed Americans the right of navigation of the Mississippi and of depositing and transferring foodstuffs at New Orleans. These were major commercial concessions. However, it also widened the breach between Federalists and Republicans and Washington signed it only with reluctance. Hamilton himself resigned office in 1795.

Despite these tensions and despite the emergence of two distinct parties in Washington's second term, Washington's presidency was to be as significant in foreign policy as in domestic. This policy, developed further by the Monroe Doctrine of 1823, left the United States neutral towards Europe after 1793 and thus able to profit from the twenty-five years of war into which Europe was plunged by the French Revolution and Napoleon. By the time that struggle was over the United States was a strong and distinct society, which could afford to be indifferent to Europe.

Nevertheless, Washington's second term was far from happy. He was distressed by the feud between his two lieutenants and by the rising spirit of party (the contemporary word was 'faction'). He was bitterly attacked in the popular press despite forty-five years of public service and found it distasteful. He made it plain in 1796 that he did not want a third term of office and this too became a precedent. Washington's farewell address was a comment and a confession. He deplored the 'baneful spirit of party', though to no avail. He stressed the need for union as 'the main prop' of American liberty, and he urged his fellow countrymen to shun foreign connections and permanent alliances. He was happy to retire at last to 'his own vine and fig tree' at Mount Vernon, where he died suddenly in 1799 from a chill caught while riding round his farms in the rain.

The presidency of John Adams

The advice of the farewell address was ignored in the bitter partisanship of the four years of John Adams' presidency (1797–1801). Since his opponent, Jefferson, had the second highest vote in the 1796 election the latter became vice-president, and thus the two leading figures in the administration were in opposite parties. What was worse, Hamilton, the leading federalist thinker and planner, conspired against Adams and had great influence over Adams' chief cabinet officers. Adams, though honest and high-minded, was vain and prickly. He, with some justice, disliked Hamilton as much as Hamilton, with less justice, disliked them. It was a miserable four years.

Adams had one achievement to his credit. Despite the tensions between the United States and revolutionary France as a result of French interference with U.S. commerce, and despite the obvious attempt by Talley-

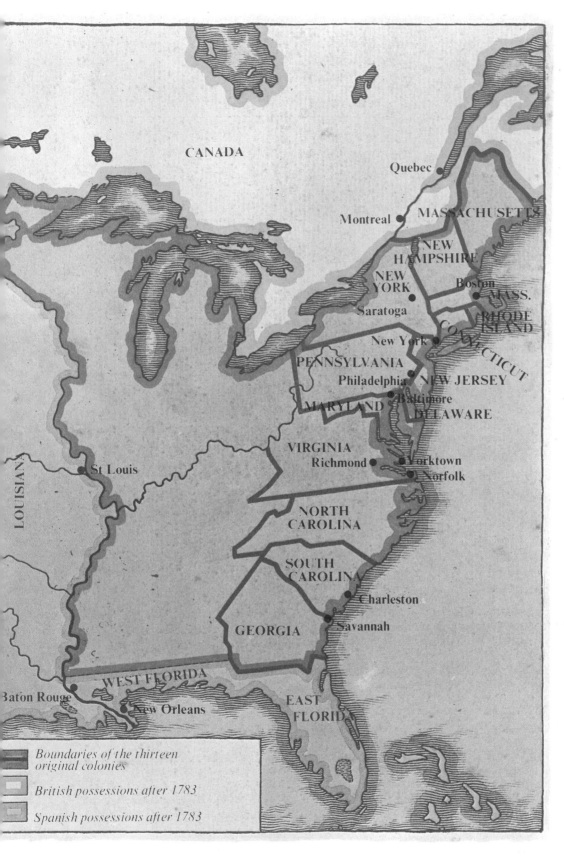

CANADA

Quebec

Montreal • MASSACHUSETTS

NEW
HAMPSHIRE

NEW
YORK • Boston • MASS.

Saratoga RHODE
ISLAND

CONNECTICUT

New York •

PENNSYLVANIA

Philadelphia • NEW JERSEY

Baltimore •
MARYLAND DELAWARE

VIRGINIA

Richmond • Yorktown
• Norfolk

NORTH
CAROLINA

SOUTH
CAROLINA

• Charleston

GEORGIA Savannah •

LOUISIANA

St Louis •

WEST FLORIDA

Baton Rouge •
New Orleans • EAST
FLORIDA

Boundaries of the thirteen
original colonies

British possessions after 1783

Spanish possessions after 1783

By the Treaty of Versailles of 1783 Britain recognised the independence of the American colonies. The red lines on the map show the boundaries of the original thirteen colonies. The larger area bounded by the orange line marks the frontier of the United States established in 1783. Under the terms of the treaty Florida, held by England since 1763, was returned to Spain, being eventually ceded by Spain to the United States in 1819. Louisiana, which was transferred from France to Spain in 1762, was returned to France in 1800 and purchased by the United States from France in 1803. Canada remained a British possession after 1783 receiving a large influx of refugees from the newly independent United States.

rand and his agents to solicit bribes from the U.S. negotiators in 1797, Adams ignored public opinion and succeeded in keeping the peace with France. However, he was unable to prevent Congress, under Federalist control, from exploiting anti-French feeling and passing in 1798 four acts that were obviously intolerant and which in the end strengthened the Republicans rather than the Federalists.

The Naturalisation Act extended the residence period of aliens seeking citizenship from five to fourteen years, thus hitting at the Republican party to which foreigners tended to flock. The Alien Act authorised the president to deport any aliens whom he considered dangerous. The Alien Enemies Act empowered him to deport the aliens of any country with which the United States

was at war. Finally, the Sedition Act made it possible to punish by fine or imprisonment anyone publishing any 'false, scandalous and malicious writing'. Under this act ten republican editors were convicted or punished.

The intent was clearly to silence all opposition and this gave Jefferson and Madison their chance. In the Kentucky and Virginia Resolutions, they set forth the Republican or states' rights view—that the federal government was created by the states and might be criticised by the states if it exceeded its powers. They claimed, in fact, that, as the constitution stated, power remained with the states or with the people. In the presidential election of 1800, Jefferson and Aaron Burr, each with 73 votes in the Electoral College, defeated Adams and Charles C. Pinckney. The final choice of president was made by the House of Representatives, which, after thirty-six acrimonious ballots, chose Jefferson.

To prevent a recurrence of such a tie in the future, the twelfth amendment was passed in 1804, to allow for the election of president and vice-president on separate ballots. Jefferson, highly cultivated, idealistic and liberal, moved into a still uncompleted presidential mansion (not yet the White House), in far from completed federal city (not yet Washington), to preside over a tenuously united United States. Nevertheless, the year 1800 marked, in mood, in direction and in consequences a real revolution.

The French Revolution

France on the verge of economic collapse; the conflicts within the Old Order; the outbreak of Revolution; the dominance of the middle classes in the National Assembly; the Revolution gains momentum; rule by the Committee of Public Safety; France at war with Europe; the reign of Terror; the radical alliance of Jacobins and sans-culottes; Robespierre supreme; the Directory—the middle classes recover their influence; the Consulate establishes the dictatorship of one man; Napoleon dominates Europe.

The French Revolution was neither the only nor the first of the disturbances that shook the old order in Europe in the late eighteenth century, but it was the most spectacular and the most important. It broke out in one of the largest, most populous and powerful of European countries, and one which was for many the very centre of culture and civilisation. In its principles and its practice it went much further than the American Revolution both politically and socially. Moreover, unlike the American Revolution, the French Revolution was propagandist and aggressive, challenging the old order outside its boundaries with armies as well as ideas.

In twenty years of war it carried revolutionary ideas throughout the length and breadth of Europe, and no place it touched was quite the same thereafter. Its influence extended even to places where its armies never set foot and persisted long after the event, and it found an echo in those movements of nationalism and democracy— liberal, radical and even socialist—which dominated so much of the politics of the following century. For generations it provided the very image or idea of revolution, for those who dreaded it as well as for those who desired it.

There is no single, simple explanation of this great episode, if only because the Revolution itself was not a single, static event. It was a dynamic series of events, whose development depended upon the interaction of a variety of forces and circumstances. Undoubtedly the most important of these factors was the middle class (*bourgeoisie*), and it is possible to see the Revolution simply as a major episode in the onward march of the conquering middle classes. They represented the new forces in society, growing in numbers, importance and ambition, and increasingly out of sympathy with the existing values and institutions (political, social and economic), which were still geared to the conditions and needs of a bygone age. They provided most of the leaders of the Revolution, the men who dominated its assemblies and committees. They compiled the indictments against the old regime, and in the 'Declaration of the Rights of Man' they proclaimed the principles of the new order. It was they who shaped the new institutions and it was they who emerged in the end as the major beneficiary of the subsequent regime.

Even so, the Revolution was not purely a battle of the middle classes against aristocracy and absolutism. Without the activity of humbler elements of society, the peasantry and the urban lower classes, the Revolution would not have followed the course it did. The fate of middle-class revolutionaries often depended on, and their policies were often conditioned by, the role of these other groups, which were driven on by discontents and aspirations which did not always coincide with those of the middle classes.

The situation, for example, which led to the summoning of the Estates-General, and which was to give the middle-class spokesmen their opportunity, was not primarily the doing of the *bourgeoisie* or its popular allies. It was the product of the difficulties of the monarchy and the ambitions of the aristocracy. By 1793 'royalists' and 'aristocrats' might appear to the popular mind as the two great enemies of the revolutionary ideals of liberty and equality, but in the 1780's the most obvious conflict in France was between the crown and the aristocracy. And it is this which explains the outbreak of revolution, even if thereafter there was a realignment of the forces involved.

The old order

The absolute monarchy of eighteenth-century France marked the peak of the crown's ascent to authority. Internal rivals to its political power had been reduced to submission in the seventeenth century. Nobles who had once challenged the crown in battle now waited on its pleasure. The palace of Versailles, the splendours of the

CÉRÉMONIE DU SACRE DE LOUIS XVI
le 11 Juin 1775.

court it housed and the royal power it symbolised—all these served as models to other continental rulers to be admired and imitated. Theories of divine right and absolutism reflected the crown's triumph. According to the absolutist theory, all the powers of the state—legislative, executive and judicial—rested with the king himself. 'It is in my person alone', said Louis XV, 'that sovereign power resides . . . it is from me alone that my courts derive their authority . . . it is to me alone that legislative power belongs completely and exclusively.'

There was no constitutional check on the king's powers, no body of elected, representative people with which he must work or to which his servants needed to answer. Hereafter, no doubt, the king would have to answer to God, but on earth he was God's agent and wielded his powers by divine right. 'The royal throne,' the seventeenth-century theologian, Bossuet, had claimed, 'is not the throne of a man but of God himself.'

By the 1770's, however, the practical weaknesses of the crown were as important as its vast theoretical claims. This was partly a matter of character. Louis XIV's successors were weaker individuals, and the administration lacked the effective direction and co-ordination which only a dedicated monarch, or a chief minister with his steadfast backing, could provide. There was moreover, a real decline in the profession of kingship (*'le métier du roi'*). But the main weakness was the chronic inadequacy of the monarchy's finances. Its money troubles were not the result of extravagant favours and pensions lavished on idle courtiers, though these were an extra burden. They were mainly the price paid for the long series of increasingly expensive wars that France had fought over the past 100 years. The annual interest due on the debts incurred in these was now swallowing about half the royal revenue. Current military costs, also an increasingly heavy item, took another quarter. It was only in peacetime, and then with luck, that the monarchy could stumble along just on the right side of bankruptcy.

The failure of reform

Financial difficulties were a symptom as well as a cause of weakness. They did not reflect any dwindling in the resources of the country, but rather the crown's inability to draw on these resources more fully, to increase them or to reorganise the tax system so as to make it more productive. Important groups and regions enjoyed privileges, exemptions in taxation and some of the more recently acquired provinces, the so-called *pays d'états,* had successfully claimed the right to negotiate their own contributions to taxation. Many towns, or groups within the towns, were either exempt from the *taille,* (the most important direct tax), or arranged to pay it on easier terms. A previous royal device for raising money— the creation and sale of offices—had by now resulted in a horde of hereditary, irremovable office-holders, exempt from certain taxes.

Indirect taxation was contracted out to private companies, the farmers-general, and the country itself was divided by a network

Above left: Louis XVI as a young man. (Bibliothèque Nationale, Paris.)

Above: pageantry marked the coronation of Louis XVI, who was kind and well intentioned, but was lacking the qualities needed in the troubles ahead. (Bibliothèque Nationale, Paris.)

of natural barriers where these customs dues and tolls were levied. The Church owned about ten per cent of the land of France and its revenues were large; but its contribution to royal revenue was limited to its own occasional 'voluntary grant'. The nobility, owning about twenty-five per cent of the land, was exempt from the *taille*, and, although not exempt from other direct taxes—the *capitation* and the *vingtième*—it often secured a favourable assessment for these. The taxes were collected efficiently enough but the drawbacks of this undergrowth of vested interest were not only that they represented a loss in revenue, but also that the tax burden bore all the more heavily on the poor, increasing their hardship and discontent. Moreover, internal customs hindered the growth of domestic commerce and the expansion of the nation's resources. In fact, the chief beneficiaries of the system of tax collection were the farmers-general themselves.

By the middle of the eighteenth century there were signs that royal ministers were fully aware of this deplorable state of affairs. There were schemes for reforming the fiscal system, for persuading the privileged classes to give up some of their tax immunities and for cutting away some of the tangle of local barriers and particular interests which restricted the growth of the nation's wealth.

However, every attempt to introduce such reform met fierce protests from the beneficiaries of privilege, especially the nobility. Tax exemptions had a monetary value which was important to many impoverished country nobles. They were a valuable mark of social status, which mattered to them all. Nor were the nobles keen to sacrifice their cherished rights to please an absolute monarchy, which had excluded them from what many considered their historic right to a share in political power. Indeed, in the eighteenth century there was an aristocratic resurgence as the nobles moved to the counter-offensive against royal absolutism. By the 1780's the crown's financial plight had become the aristocracy's opportunity.

The power of the *parlements*

The main spokesmen of the resistance to reforms and of the attack on absolutism were the *parlements*, especially the *Parlement* of Paris, the most important of a dozen in the kingdom. They were essentially courts of law and the special preserve of the judicial aristocracy, the *noblesse de robe*. In one important respect their powers were more than judicial: all royal decrees had to be registered with them and they could present protests before registration took place. Although the king could then override their protests, these were nevertheless an important weapon of resistance, and one used to great effect. Any scheme which affected privilege called forth the protests of the *parlements*.

With the co-operation of the local estates in Brittany and Languedoc and the assembly of the clergy they thwarted moves for more fiscal equality in the early 1750's and again in 1763. During the 1760's they backed the estates of Brittany in a long resistance to the royal representative. In the course of this conflict they asserted that only the Estates-General, the old assembly which had not met since 1614, could ratify new taxes. Louis XV, in a burst of energy during his last years, had overriden the *parlements* and then suppressed them so that his ministers could get on with reform programmes. However, Louis XVI, in one of the first and most misguided acts of his reign, restored the *parlements*. They then resumed their campaign of obstruction up until 1788.

The effect of this conduct on the part of the *parlements* was not only to thwart useful reforms and prop up the system of privilege, but also to bring absolutism into growing disrepute. Although their resistance was inspired by petty self-interest, they presented it as the defence of liberty, constitutionalism and law against the onslaught of a despotic crown. When the king set their objections on one side, and still more when he suspended the *parlements*, it merely seemed further evidence of the tyranny in action.

The terms in which they framed their protests helped to make familiar, notions of limited monarchy, representative institutions, fundamental laws and the rights of the nation. Their own interpretation of these was, in fact, narrow: liberty meant their privileges and representative institutions a body dominated by the nobility. Yet they were liked by the common people. This was partly due to skilful publicity and well-organised demonstrations, but it was also because the attack on despotism struck a popular note. Liberty and representative institutions, although in a wider sense than the *parlements* contemplated, had attractions for many outside the privileged orders.

The social order

In this political conflict the aristocracy might feel that popular opinion was with them against despotism. Social discontent, on the other hand, made for a different alignment of forces.

Society under the old regime was still essentially aristocratic: prestige and pre-eminence in the social hierarchy were accorded to those of noble birth or possessing titled rank and landed estates. These distinctions enjoyed official legal recognition in the traditional concept of society as consisting of three estates: the clergy, the nobility and the rest, the first two orders being entitled to special privileges.

Some of the nobility's privileges were honorific, like the right to carry a sword. More materially, they were exempt from paying the *taille* and favoured in other aspects of direct taxation. A noble landowner was entitled as *seigneur* to exercise

jurisdiction in manorial courts and to retain the fines imposed. He was also allowed to hold certain monopolies in his manor, such as the winepress, whose users had to pay him a fee. Finally, he was entitled to a variety of feudal dues, in the shape of money payments—some annual and some occasional—as well as services from the peasantry.

Within the nobility there were differences and distinctions, such as those between the few thousand great ones who frequented the royal court at Versailles and the lesser, often hard pressed, provincial nobles. There was a further distinction between the older nobility 'of the sword' and the office-holding, judicial nobility 'of the robe'. But by contrast with all non-nobles, the small group of perhaps 400,000 had this distinction in common: all held by law a superior, privileged position in society.

There were signs, especially from the mid-eighteenth century, that they were maintaining this position more exclusively and exploiting it more thoroughly. The *parlements* tried to restrict entry into their ranks to those who were already of noble descent. From 1781 most commissions in the army were open only to those who could prove that they stemmed from generations of nobility. They appropriated more and more of the better posts which had before been open to non-nobles, especially those with money. By the 1780's all the bishops, all the intendants (provincial administrators) and almost every one of the royal ministers were nobles. In the countryside, perhaps under the pressure of rising costs of living, they began to exploit their seigneurial rights more strongly, even to the extent of resurrecting old, unenforced ones and claiming payment of arrears.

The rise of the *bourgeoisie*

The Third Estate, the non-privileged order, comprised more than ninety-five per cent of the French population. They were not nobles and they were not clergy but they might be anything else. The Third Estate was a legal category and not a social or economic class. The wealthiest and most progressive element covered a wide and ill-defined range of comfortably off townsmen. They flourished especially in such activities as finance, commerce and industry, administration and the liberal professions. They were the chief beneficiaries of the remarkable commercial expansion of France during the eighteenth century.

Between the 1720's and 1780's foreign trade had trebled, colonial trade multiplied five times, industrial output doubled, prices rose and profit margins increased. The great ports of Marseilles, Nantes and Bordeaux enjoyed an unprecedented prosperity. In towns and cities a rush of building projects—elegant town houses, public squares and gardens, promenades and parks—bore witness to the new wealth. Only big financiers, organising the loans for central and local

authorities, or the great tax farmers could outdo in fortune the merchant-princes of the foreign and colonial trade.

Industry, like domestic trade, suffered from the hindrances that impeded economic activity under the old regime—the internal tariff barriers, government regulations and guild restrictions. Even so, large-scale enterprises based mainly on a domestic system rather than mechanisation, were appearing.

The administrative and professional groups, the holders of small offices in the courts and the bureaucracies, and the lawyers, doctors and writers, could not match the wealth of the businessman, but they were far more numerous and included a mass of talent—educated, articulate, enlightened and ambitious. From this section more than any other came the leadership in the Revolution, the men who dominated its assemblies and committees, shaped its legislation and conducted its policies.

These middle classes, growing in size and wealth and conscious of their importance to the country, were not likely to tolerate indefinitely old systems, institutions and values which barred them from a share in power, hindered their freedom of industry, restricted economic enterprise and relegated them to an inferior social status. Yet they were slow to act in independent opposition to the privileged orders. Many of them not

only aspired to reach these social heights themselves, but for a long time had enjoyed opportunities to do so. The crown had often drawn its servants from these sections of society rather than from the feudal nobility. Wealthy *bourgeois* had benefited from the royal practice of creating offices for sale, for these could confer noble status. They might marry their children into the families of needy nobles, or use their wealth to get their son a promising position in the judiciary or the administration. They might buy land together with seigneurial rights and to that extent live like lords.

From the mid-eighteenth century the growing exclusiveness of the nobility hindered advance through these traditional channels and probably increased social resentment. Everywhere, according to the politician Antoine Barnave, privilege barred the path to all but trivial careers. Georges Danton complained of a system which gave educated men no opportunity to show their talents. Even so, the injured self-esteem and frustrated ambition of the middle classes were slow to transform themselves into weapons of revolution. Only when it became apparent that the aims of the aristocracy did not include any abandoning of their privileged position, did the middle classes break away and strike out on their own.

The townspeople and the peasants

Below the minority of comfortable *bourgeoisie* came the vast majority of townsfolk. In Paris they accounted for well over 400,000 of the city's population of half a million. They ranged from small tradesmen and shopkeepers, workshop masters, craftsmen and journeymen down to labourers and domestic servants, paupers and vagrants. These were the common people, a collection of small-income groups including wage-earners. There was little development as yet of a distinct wage-earning proletariat and virtually no organisation of workers.

Most workshops were on a very small scale. Masters, themselves craftsmen, worked alongside their few employees and

Above: on 10 *May* 1774, *a great pageant was organised to salute the new king Louis XVI on his formal entry into Versailles, the show-place built by Louis XIV. The palace became a model which all European rulers tried to copy. (Bibliothèque Nationale, Paris.)*

journeymen often lodged with their masters. Masters and men together resisted the attacks of big employers on the guild regulations which protected the crafts. As small earners, whatever their activity they easily felt the pinch of rising prices, especially of bread, and their normal collective response to this was not strikes and wage demands, but food riots, calls for price controls and action to improve the town's supplies of grain. In this respect they lived in a different world from the *bourgeoisie*, who were strangers to this kind of economic distress.

Most Frenchmen, however, were not townsmen at all. More than eighty per cent of the population were rural and the great majority of them were peasants. They were free individuals—there was very little serfdom left in France—and in this respect they were better off than the peasantry of many other countries. Many of them, perhaps a quarter, had come to own their land. Others

were tenant-farmers on a rent or sharecropping basis. Many (in Normandy perhaps thirty per cent), were little more than landless labourers. Except in the case of a fortunate minority their conditions, even if better than at earlier times, were oppressive. Even those who held land had so little that they needed to supplement their earnings. Most got little benefit from the rising prices of foodstuffs, since few had much surplus for sale. The population rose by about 6,000,000 (or thirty per cent) during the eighteenth century, and this increased the competition for land, encouraged the sub-division of holdings, swelled the ranks of the landless and checked advances in wages. In addition, the peasants bore the full weight of royal taxes—the *taille* and the salt tax. They paid tithes to the Church and dues to the lord of the manor. They also faced increasingly heavy pressure from those with a more commercial approach to agriculture. Progressive

Left: the French fleet fired a salute to honour the emperor Joseph II when he visited Toulon. (Musée de la Marine, Paris.) Bottom: the king inspecting the new fortifications at Cherbourg. (Musée de la Marine, Paris.)

landlords threatened to depress the poorer peasantry still further by enclosing common land and by depriving them of traditional rights, however desirable this might be for agrarian advance. Finally, their *seigneurs* squeezed harder for feudal dues—the most detested burden of all, as the complaints and conduct of the peasants in 1789 were to show.

These discontents acquired an additional significance with the growth of public discussion of critical ideas about man, government and country. The *philosophes*, whose writings provided much of the material for discussion in salons, literary clubs and philosophical societies, were concerned with far more than politics, and their political notions did not always agree. Not revolutionaries in the normal sense, they nevertheless encouraged a revolution of rising expectations and helped to undermine confidence in the existing order. Inspired by the triumph of physical science in discovering the grand, simple laws of nature, they favoured a similar rational approach, questioning all traditional beliefs, customs and institutions. Their writings preached and encouraged this critical attitude.

Their chief target was the Church as the stronghold of irrational belief and superstition, insisting on blind, unquestioning obedience to apparently absurd dogmas, and preventing by censorship and persecution the spread or even the holding of other opinions. The powerful attacks by the *philosophes* on this bulwark of tradition helped to weaken the hold of traditionalism in general. Above all they were concerned with freedom, the essential condition of the better society they hoped for: freedom to question, to hold opinions and to communicate them by speech and writing. In conditions of freedom rational man, as they understood him, seemed capable of great achievements.

Louis XVI

The reform of institutions from above would not have been impossible, but it would have been extremely difficult. The crown would have had to prove itself a despot equipped with a vigour and ruthlessness of which it had as yet given no evidence, in order to rouse feelings against it. Moreover, the 'despot' would need to be magnanimous enough to admit limitations on his own authority.

All this called for a mixture of authority and finesse, in which the new king, who came to the throne in 1774, was sadly lacking. Louis XVI was a well-meaning young man who wanted to be liked. He had simple tastes and was not very fond of the glittering round of court life. Rather shy and awkward, fat and not very lively, he preferred the harmless pleasures of eating, hunting or tinkering at his work bench. He would have done well, Madame Roland thought, in some obscure position in life. The business of government and administration bored him. He lacked the strength of character to stand by a subordinate, against the untiring pressures, intrigues and influences around him. He showed no personal initiative of his own at all.

His queen, Marie Antoinette, was shallow and fickle and did nothing to offset his weaknesses. She had many enemies, through no fault of her own, but her indiscreet behaviour gave them opportunities for campaigns against her which lowered still further the reputation and popularity of the monarchy.

The work of Turgot

Louis XVI's earliest actions, designed to show his goodwill, were misguided. He brought back the *parlements* and dismissed the ministers who had got rid of them. This was a popular move but it proved disastrous for the prospects of reform. It cancelled out the otherwise promising appointment of Turgot as controller-general of finance. Turgot was a devoted servant of the crown, an experienced administrator who had achieved impressive results as intendant of Limoges and a disciple of progressive economic thought. He believed that the way to increase national wealth was to abolish the internal barriers which limited the circulation of goods, and the restrictions which hampered industrial enterprise. He also believed that the way to improve royal finances was to make all landed proprietors pay taxes. His measures embodied this: he freed the internal market in grain, abolished the privileges of the guilds and substituted a general tax on land for the peasants' obligation to do road work. He transformed an annual deficit of 21,000,000 *livres* into a surplus of 11,000,000.

The opposition to these reforms was fierce. The *parlements* protested, declaring that Turgot's attack on privilege threatened the whole existing social structure. Louis ignored them, but the vested interests persisted in their opposition. The queen's circle murmured against Turgot; other ministers undermined his position. Despite Turgot's pleas to Louis to hold firm, to stand by him and to ride out the storm, Louis dismissed him in 1776. In doing so he sacrificed his best, if not his last, opportunity. Turgot was quick of tongue and temper, but he had ability and integrity, and these were qualities in short supply in 1776.

In the next confrontation with the privileged opposition, the crown's needs were once more desperate and its position more precarious than ever. Within ten years the monarchy was bankrupt, and its weakness was the aristocracy's opportunity to force its demands for a share in power.

The crucial development was the French intervention in the American Revolution. The French government obtained what it had sought since 1763—revenge for its defeat by Britain in the Seven Years' War. It was, however, to prove the most expensive act of vengeance in French history. This was partly because association with the American cause stimulated the fashionable notions of liberty and representative government. Much more important was its shattering effect on the weak royal finances.

Jacques Necker

Turgot's successor as director of the Treasury was Jacques Necker, a Swiss banker. Since he was a Protestant he was not made controller-general of finance or a member of the royal council. Necker financed the war from loans, raised often at eight or ten per cent interest. This not only sent the total debt soaring, but required an even greater share of the annual revenue for paying the interest due on the debts. The charges had more than doubled since 1774, and were swallowing more than half the state income. An annual budget deficit had never been unusual, but it was now more than double the deficit which Turgot had faced.

Retrenchment would make little impression on this, nor could borrowing go on at such a rate. Moreover, existing taxes could not be fruitfully increased, especially since the economy had slumped since the late 1770's and those whose tax burden was already heavy were suffering a decline in real wages. The only solution was to recast the tax system so that all paid, regardless of status. The sole fiscal reform which would meet the crown's needs inevitably involved an attack on the existing social system of privileged orders.

This was the essence of the programme proposed by Calonne, who was controller-general from 1783 to 1787. The ending of the American War hid the real position for a time as did an excellent harvest and a trade treaty with Britain. For a time Calonne lived in a false boom, built roads and harbours, and raised big loans. In 1786, however, he reverted to Turgot's policy. He proposed to replace the *vingtième*, in which the nobility were favoured, with a new tax on all land regardless of the status of its owner. To stimulate productivity internal barriers were to be abolished. There were to be new local assemblies to help advise in taxation, which would be based on land-owning, not social status: wealth, not birth and rank, would be the measure. Moreover, they were to be controlled by the royal agent, the intendant.

The new tax would ease the crown's finances, by providing a permanent broad-based tax on all land. The composition of the new assemblies would check the social exclusiveness and political pretensions of the privileged nobility. They would also give greater opportunities to wealthy, local middle-class men to play a role. They would increase the efficiency and uniformity of administration and they would, under the intendants, be acting as agencies of the

crown. At the same time the removal of economic barriers would at once promote a greater unity within the kingdom and provide more incentives to economic enterprise.

The retreat from absolutism

For these same reasons the policies could expect opposition from both the defenders of the existing system and the critics of royal despotism. Calonne hoped to avoid this by summoning a hand-picked assembly of notables drawn from the high nobility, the men of the *parlements* and the leading clergy. If careful explanation and persuasion could win their approval beforehand, subsequent opposition from the *parlements* might be less automatic and less effective.

The notables disappointed these hopes. Some were ready to give up their tax privileges, but even they were not convinced of the need for new taxes, nor were they keen on assemblies which ignored distinctions between the three estates and looked like institutions to strengthen the ministerial authority. When Calonne tried to appeal to a wider public, he lost whatever influence he had had with these notables, and Louis was persuaded to dismiss him.

Calonne's successor, Loménie de Brienne, an ambitious cleric and one of Calonne's leading critics in the Assembly of Notables, had no more success. For all his criticism of Calonne, Brienne's own proposals were only a slightly modified version of his predecessor's. Despite Brienne's standing with the notables, the Church and the queen, his proposals were rejected. The notables had done nothing to relieve the financial position. By defending privilege and the status quo they had angered the Third Estate. Real reform could come only from some higher body, preferably the Estates-General, which had last met in 1614.

Thwarted in his first approach, Brienne turned next to the traditional method: he brought forward his decrees to be registered by the *Parlement* of Paris. The result of this was the appearance in full force of the revolt of the nobility. The two driving forces in the *Parlement*, the one concerned to preserve privilege and the other aspiring to a check on despotism by constitutional means had both been encouraged by the rebuffs already delivered to the monarchy by the notables. They refused to register the tax proposals and demanded the summoning of the Estates-General as the one body competent to agree to a tax on land. Months of conflict came to a head in May 1788. The *Parlement* issued a manifesto denouncing arbitrary government, arrest and taxation, and asserting the rights of the Estates-General in matters of taxation. Brienne sent troops, arrested leaders, had all the *parlements* suspended and proposed to transfer their powers of legislation and appeal to a new set of tribunals.

Far from settling matters, this act provoked the biggest demonstrations witnessed so far. The *parlements* were seen—far from accurately—as a barrier against tyranny. In Paris and the provinces the despotism of ministers was denounced. The Assembly of the Clergy protested, as did the leading nobles. Hundreds of pamphlets appeared championing the Paris *Parlement*. Riots broke out in provincial cities. In Brittany, where provincial feeling was always strong and the local Estates were flourishing, the machinery of resistance was highly organised. Elsewhere, as in Dauphiné, where the local Estates had long since died out, campaigns were begun to restore them. At Grenoble popular riots prevented troops

The ancient regime (that is the old order before the Revolution) was, for a privileged few, a world of affluence and leisure. Above left: the Prince of Conti's family at dinner. (Musée de Versailles.) The king for his part, had simple tastes and this equestrian portrait (above) hardly suggests a dedicated soldier. (Musée de Versailles.) He was happiest when hunting or tinkering at his bench as a locksmith or (bottom left) strolling in the fields. (Bibliothèque Nationale, Paris.)

from removing the local *parlement*, and a hastily summoned provincial Estates refused to pay the new taxes until these were sanctioned by the Estates-General.

Faced with this widespread protest the government gave in. The notion of new tribunals, along with other projected reforms, was abandoned. Brienne resigned and was replaced by Necker; his last act was, in fact, to declare the nation bankrupt. The crown agreed to summon, in May 1789, the Estates-General. In September 1788 the *Parlement* of Paris was restored amid popular acclaim. The privileged classes, with wide popular support from members of the Third Estate, had forced absolutism to retreat. To accept the Estates-General was to admit the right of a representative body to a share in power and thus to a permanent limitation in the authority of the crown. However, the successful aristocratic revolt to end the autocratic power of the crown had merely opened the way to a revolution that was to end the power of the privileged aristocracy. As the French writer, François de Chateaubriand, later said: 'the patricians began the Revolution and the plebeians completed it.'

The Third Estate

The common front of nobility and commoners against absolutism had hardly won its victory in the summer of 1788 when it began to disintegrate. The reason for this was the Third Estate's discovery that the nobility's intentions were very different from its own. Once it became apparent that the nobility's idea of a constitution was one which ensured its own predominance and perpetuated the existing system of inequality of status, the Third Estate denounced its former allies and struck out on its own. 'Despotism and constitution', wrote an observer, 'are now minor questions. The war is between the Third Estate and the other two orders.'

There had already been signs of this division of interests, notably in Brittany, even at the height of the common resistance to Brienne. But the great revelation of how narrow the aristocracy's aspirations were came with the announcement by the *Parlement* of Paris, just after its restoration, that the Estates-General should meet in its ancient form. Each Estate was to return the same number of representatives, each was to meet separately and each was to vote separately.

This would condemn the Third Estate to permanent inferiority and impotence. Since two of the three orders were privileged, vote by order would mean that the Third Estate could always be outvoted by two to one and certainly would be on anything which touched the privileged status of the other two Estates. Royal absolutism would be exchanged for a constitution dominated by privileged orders. In seconding the nobility's demands for a constitution, the middle

50

classes had not meant to revive a medieval relic which would perpetuate the concept of stratified estates and enshrine their own inferiority. They added to the protest against absolutism their own clamour against privileged status. The Revolution was to be about equality as well as liberty.

The indignation at the Paris *Parlement's* announcement was immediate and widespread. The *parlements* lost their traditional popularity, and the privileged orders in general became the major target of denunciation. In a great outpouring of pamphlets and petitions the Third Estate proclaimed its own ideas and demands. These were that the Third Estate should have as many representatives as the clergy and nobility together (the 'doubling of the Third'), that all the orders should meet in a single assembly and that voting should be by individuals, with the decision going by majorities. In such a mixed assembly the Third Estate would be powerful, since its representatives could expect support from the more liberal nobles and from the poorer clergy.

The general mood is well illustrated in the best-known of these pamphlets, *What is the Third Estate* by the Abbé Siéyès. It was useless, he said, for the Third to be represented under the ancient forms: 'Its presence would only consecrate the oppression of which it must be the eternal victim.' It would prolong the 'odious injustice' whereby, whatever a man's talent, industry and public service, the path to honours and high position would stay closed to him, and be open only to the privileged orders. He went further when he dismissed the aristocracy as a tiny (and useless) minority. The Third Estate represented the nation: 24,000,000 commoners mattered more than 400,000 of the privileged. The Third Estate was 'everything'. So far it had been treated in practice as if it were 'nothing'. It demanded in future to count for something.

There were the beginnings also of organisation to promote the Third Estate's views. Liberal aristocrats like Lafayette, enlightened *parlement*. Men like Adrien Duport and Hérault de Séchelles, clerics like Talleyrand and Siéyès, and even princes of the blood like the Duc d'Orléans associated with the 'patriotic' party.

One request, for the doubling of the Third Estate's representation, was conceded by the king in December 1788. He did not say whether the orders should sit and vote together, but it seemed as if the crown were coming down on the side of the Third Estate's demands.

The meeting of the Estates-General

The preparations for the coming assembly of the Estates-General added to the air of excitement and expectation. In thousands of meetings throughout France men assembled to elect the representatives of their order for their district and to discuss and draft the lists of grievances (*cahiers*) they would take with them to Versailles. The nobility, like the clergy, chose their representatives directly, but the deputies for the Third Estate were chosen indirectly. Most Frenchmen over the age of twenty-five could vote in a local assembly but they usually picked electors who proceeded to a higher meeting of electors which actually chose the deputies.

This process favoured the men of some eloquence, education and local standing, especially as these same meetings had to discuss and draft the list of grievances. It favoured the urban, professional middle class: men like Maximilien Robespierre in Artois, and Antoine Barnave and Jean Mounier in Dauphiné. Of the 610 deputies, about two-thirds were lesser office-holders or lawyers, and another five per cent came from other professions. About thirteen per cent were from commerce, manufacture or finance and about ten per cent were farmers.

The general list of grievances of the Third Estate was mainly the work of this middle-class group. Some of the demands of the peasantry and poorer people were neglected or glossed over. But they do reveal the line of divergence between the middle classes and the privileged orders. The grievances submitted by all the orders usually denounced arbitrary government, demanded a constitution, a representative body to control taxation, freedom of the individual and the press, and the abolition of internal customs barriers. But the nobility, though sometimes ready to give up its tax exemptions, still insisted on its honorific privileges and on its special status—the retention of the system of separate orders. For its part the Third Estate demanded complete civil equality: the nobility was to lose all its privileges and its special status.

There was in all this another opportunity for the king. The alliance of people and nobility had broken down. The groups which had so often sabotaged ministerial plans for reform, were unpopular with the spokesmen of the Third Estate. By his

Top left: revolutionary justice was horrifying for the ladies of easy virtue since the Jacobins grounded their notions of political reform on a puritan spirit. The women of the streets had their heads shaven before being imprisoned in St. Lazare, a jail reserved for them. (Bibliothèque Nationale, Paris.)
Left: on the Champs de Mars the inhabitants of the Palais Royal were later to demonstrate, in order to show their revolutionary sentiments; but under the old regime it was still a place for promenades and gossip. (Bibliothèque Nationale, Paris.)
Far left: a young Frenchwoman wearing a Revolutionary costume. (Bibliothèque Nationale, Paris.)

did not mark the conversion of Louis to their ideas, but merely a temporary expedient. Recalcitrant nobles and court circles were urging him to use force. He began to summon regiments to Paris and Versailles. He dismissed Necker and replaced him with a court favourite, the Baron de Breteuil. It looked as if the last argument of kings was to be used against the upstart deputies. What saved the day for the National Assembly was the appearance of new forces in this complex movement. And these forces had their own interests and aspirations which made them invaluable but disturbing and uncertain supporters of the middle class in the Assembly.

The beginning of the Revolution

It was the intervention of the people of Paris that thwarted any royal plan for using force. This was not merely a gesture of solidarity. Economic distress caused by high prices and shortage of food was particularly

agreement to meet a representative body in order to discuss reform and by his concession which enabled the representation of the Third Estate to be doubled, Louis had won popularity and trust. An alliance of crown and people on a basis of moderate reform was feasible. But it was expecting a great deal of a monarch whose whole upbringing and outlook were cast in a traditional mould to throw over the nobility and join with a collection of provincial lawyers and bureaucrats. It was too much for a monarch as indecisive as Louis XVI, who was surrounded by influences favouring the established system.

The defiance of the Third Estate

As the Estates-General assembled in May 1789, the hopeful deputies of the Third Estate were soon disillusioned. The traditional ceremonies underlined their inferior status: they had to wear black, enter by a side door and go bareheaded, while the other orders wore hats. They were received in a different room. When Necker announced that the Estates should meet separately, not in a common assembly, disillusion was complete. On this vital point the king had agreed with the privileged orders.

Recognising that to accept this was to accept the defeat of their hopes, the deputies of the Third Estate determined to ignore it. They embarked on a tactic of passive resistance and began a war of nerves. They refused to take any step, however small, until the other orders should join them. For weeks no business at all was transacted. On the 17th June they went further and took a

clearly revolutionary step: they proclaimed themselves to be, not the mere representatives of the Third Estate, but the National Assembly. On the 20th June, finding their normal meeting hall locked, they adjourned to a nearby tennis court and took an oath not to disperse till a constitution had been finally established.

On the 23rd June they carried their defiance still further. Louis, addressing all the orders in a special session, outlined important reforms but said that the ancient distinction of the three orders would be preserved in its entirety and ordered the estates to assemble in their separate halls the next day. The deputies of the Third Estate sat firm. 'The nation when assembled,' declared Jean Bailly, the president of the Third Estate, 'cannot be given orders'. 'We will not leave our places', said Mirabeau, 'except at the point of a bayonet'. Many of the clergy including the Archbishop of Paris (from fear) and Talleyrand, bishop of Autun (from calculated enthusiasm) had already responded to the Third Estate's exhortations to join them. So did about forty of the nobles, including the Duc d'Orléans. Louis, perhaps alarmed at the growth of unrest in Paris, yielded. On June 27th he instructed the First and Second Estates to merge with the National Assembly. The Third Estate had won its war of nerves with the king and the nobility. Henceforth, there were no representatives of the Estates of France, only representatives of the French nation.

Despite their impressive defiance the position of the middle-class deputies remained precarious. The royal orders of 27th June

acute. The price of bread in Paris was double the normal rate. Wide popular unrest over this had shown itself in demonstrations, so that when the political crisis of July arose the Parisian people were already in the streets in an angry mood. Feelings about politics might not have brought them out in such strength or worked on them with such effect, had it not been for these economic grievances. Time and again during the Revolution food shortages and rising prices would appear as the great driving force behind popular discontent. Yet, although high prices could provoke riots, these would have had no more significance than they had had in the past, but for the political situation.

The Parisians were kept in touch with the latest developments as news and rumours came through from Versailles. The great distributing centre was the Palais Royal, a favourite public resort, where every night orators and agitators including, in particular, Camille Desmoulins, addressed the crowds. They warned the people of aristo-

cratic schemes to launch troops against Paris and urged them to take up arms. Excited and alarmed, the crowds surged through the streets seeking weapons, which they found in the Hôtel de Ville and the Hôtel des Invalides.

On July 14th they converged on the Bastille in the Faubourg St Antoine. It was thought to contain weapons. Also it was suspect as the stronghold from which the royal troops would attack and its guns were trained on the streets. In panic the small garrison opened fire. The angry crowd, supported by rebellious soldiers with artillery, forced the governor De Launay to surrender and killed him. 'This is a revolt', said the king. 'Sire', replied a courtier, 'it is not a revolt, it is a revolution.'

The fall of the Bastille had important consequences. The king had lost control of Paris. At the same time, the body of electors who had chosen the deputies for Paris and had continued to meet thereafter, threw out the old city authorities and set up themselves as the municipal council—the Commune.

They established a militia, the National Guard, both to resist any aristocratic plots and to check excessive popular disturbances. Its commander was Lafayette; its badge the tricolour.

Throughout the towns of France similar new bodies took over from the old authorities, and set up similar national guards. Meanwhile, on July 17th the king had recalled Necker and had visited Paris where at the Town Hall he accepted the national cockade: the red and blue of Paris with the white of the Bourbons in between. The most intransigent nobles began to flee from France.

Unrest in the countryside

The same month another popular force made its weight felt in the Revolution. In the years before 1789 the position of the masses of the peasantry had worsened, with the growing pressure of population and the more rigorous exaction by *seigneurs* of their dues. In the economic recession and the bad harvests of 1788 the peasantry suffered badly, and the surviving lists of grievances of rural assemblies indicate the nature of their many complaints: enclosing landlords, tithes, heavy taxes, and above all, the seigneurial dues.

From early in 1789 there was widespread unrest and attacks on grain stores and convoys took place. The peasants had expected good news from Versailles and when none came rumours spread: the aristocrats were not only conspiring to prevent improvements but they were planning to launch armed vengeance against the peasants, and the instruments of the aristocrats were to be the brigands. This legend was strengthened by the movement of unemployed labourers and vagabonds. Such rumours spread like wildfire creating panic among the peasantry over large areas. The 'great fear' resulted in a wave of peasant uprisings, in which they attacked *châteaux*, destroyed the manorial records of the detested seigneurial dues and overturned enclosures. Many believed, or pretended to believe, that they were acting in the king's name.

The middle classes in the Assembly were alarmed. Such widespread disorders and attacks on property were not to their taste. Yet they had no forces which could put down disorders on such a scale. The only way to restore peace to the countryside was to make swift concessions. This was the underlying reason for the destruction of the feudal regime by the Assembly on August 4th. One deputy proposed the surrender of feudal rights and an orgy of sacrifice followed, as one after another tax privileges, tithes, seigneurial rights, and the privileges of provinces and cities, guilds and corporations were offered up. It was an impressive occasion, but essentially it was the recognition of an accomplished fact. Indeed, the Assembly later stipulated that the peasants

to petition the king and Assembly for bread. Several thousand women made the twelve-mile journey. The Assembly arranged that their petition for bread should reach the king, and suggested that political demands —his assent to their decrees—be added. Further persuasion appeared in the shape of 20,000 Parisian National Guards under Lafayette, presenting the demand of the Paris Commune that Louis should return to Paris. On October 6th, accompanied by cheering crowds, Louis made the journey from Versailles, to be followed in a few days by the National Assembly.

'It is finished' wrote Desmoulins. 'The aristos are at their last gasp, the patriots have triumphed.' It was not finished and Desmoulins would not live to see the end. The alliance of the middle-class Assembly and the common people of Paris was to prove uneasy and unstable. Indeed, the Assembly in Paris soon took severe measures, including the imposition of martial law, to check the excessive energies of the people.

Nevertheless, Desmoulin's optimism was understandable. The aristocracy's plans for the future of the constitution and of society had been defeated; their attempts to bring in armed force had been thwarted; and many of them had fled the country. The Assembly, backed, however fortuitously, by the people, had triumphed. The king was in Paris under their eyes. The people were calm, partly because of sterner disciplinary measures but also because the Assembly improved the flow of food to Paris and because the next harvest was good. They could proceed to reshape the institutions of France along the lines of middle-class aspirations.

should redeem the seigneurial dues. But this could never be enforced. Just as the action of townspeople throughout France had thrust aside the municipal authorities of the old regime, so the action of the peasantry had destroyed some of the traditional structure in the countryside.

The power of the common people

Yet another popular movement in Paris during October set the seal on the revolutionary triumphs of 1789. Once again it was brought about by a combination of economic distress and political excitement. The latter sprang from revived suspicions of the king's intentions. Louis had stubbornly refused to give his assent to the decrees in which the Assembly had embodied their abolition of

feudalism on August 4th. Some deputies felt he needed another push. Their impatience was reinforced by alarm early in October, when a regiment was called to Versailles and at a welcoming banquet drank royal toasts and trampled on the tricolour cockade. The orators of the Palais Royal were quick to pass on this ominous news to their excitable audiences, and to suggest thwarting such aristocratic plots by removing Louis from the poisonous atmosphere of Versailles to the pure patriotic air of Paris.

The food shortages had not been eased. There were riots and angry denunciations of the authorities, especially by the housewives of Paris. It was in the course of a demonstration by the women at the Hôtel de Ville that someone suggested they march to Versailles

The National Assembly

Between 1789 and 1791 the National Constituent Assembly carried through a great reconstruction of French institutions. Not all its measures were permanent or satisfactory: some worked poorly; some were quickly abandoned. The decision-makers were essentially men of the middle classes, who dominated the Assembly, together with some 'patriotic' nobles and clergy. For this reason their vision was often limited to the boundaries of a comfortable middle-class liberalism. Nevertheless, much of what ultimately survived from the Revolution was the work of these years, and it represented a radical change in France.

In its 'Declaration of the Rights of Man and Citizen' (August 1789), the Assembly proclaimed the principles on which the new order should be based and rejected those of the old Regime. Liberty and Equality—'men are born and remain free and equal in rights'—was the negation of arbitrary government and aristocratic privilege. Social distinctions were to be based on public usefulness only, not on inherited status. Public offices were to be open to all on a basis of talent, not reserved for a privileged few on a basis of rank. There was to be freedom of opinion, of speech and writing, and freedom from arbitrary arrest and imprisonment. Popular sovereignty—'the source of all sovereignty resides in the nation'—was a total reversal of the previous theory of royal sovereignty.

These principles, though fatal to the old order, were not meant to imply extreme measures of democracy in the new era. Equality meant equality before the law and a career open to talents, not a levelling out of economic inequalities. The fact that men had a natural right to property did not foreshadow some great redistribution: it meant that the individual property owner had a right not to be deprived of it. When the Assembly did contravene this 'sound and inviolable right', it was always with excuses and usually resulted in compensation for the affected person. Nor did popular sovereignty mean universal suffrage. The Assembly wanted to keep power in responsible, educated, middle-class hands. Hence, while all citizens enjoyed civil rights, only those paying a certain sum in taxation were classed as 'active citizens' and given the right to vote in national or local elections. Even most of the 'active' citizens could vote only in primary assemblies, the election of deputies coming at a later stage and being confined to voters with a higher tax qualification. Some deputies, notably Robespierre, protested at this creation of a new aristocracy of wealth and obtained some modifications, but the main distinctions remained.

The Assembly's reforms

In a variety of measures the Assembly carried through the destruction of the old regime which was implied in their declaration. Decrees like those of August 1789 swept away large numbers of the old privileges in shoals. The National Assembly was to a certain extent merely recognising facts already accomplished by the peasantry.

Le Serment de Reconciliation des trois Ordres.

All the authorities were too short of money to carry out effectively their administrative responsibilities. Moreover, there were conflicts between the departmental authorities and those of the communes: in the former, indirect elections produced councils of more wealthy and cautious citizens, whereas in the communes direct election in a small area produced more radical, lower-middle-class councillors. In their desire to avoid the objectionable centralisation of earlier days, the Assembly established no clear links between the local authorities and the central government. In time, however, under pressure of emergency, strong links were forged, and the leaders of France then had an administrative machine which could carry their commands through France with an efficiency no absolute monarch had ever known.

In their judicial reforms the Assembly achieved a notable success. The old system had been chaotic and confused, with a variety of courts ranging from the seigneurial courts and special ones like the ecclesiastical courts to the sovereign courts—the *parlements*. All, including the *parlements*, were swept aside. A simpler, uniform system of courts, geared to the new local government units, replaced them. The new judges and justices of the peace were to be elected. Again privilege suffered, for many of these courts had been the embodiment of privilege. Venal judicial offices were abolished, although compensation was to be paid.

They defined some seigneurial rights as legitimate property rights which the peasants should purchase from the lord. However, since the peasantry never recognised this fine distinction, in practice a great host of feudal and seigneurial dues, and obligations and payments were abolished. Serfdom was also abolished where it still lingered on. All tax privileges and exemptions of provinces, towns and corporations as well as privileged groups were suppressed, as were tithes. Hereditary nobility and titles were abolished: all men were now citizens. The old venal offices were swept away (a generous gesture from an Assembly nearly half of whose members held such offices), although all holders were to be compensated for their loss. The old *parlements* were abolished and the judges compensated for the loss of proprietary rights in their seats.

Among the most radical and enduring of the institutional changes was the reform of local government. The Assembly struck at the most disagreeable characteristics of its old structure. Local government was a con-

fused patchwork of complicated divisions, overlapping authorities, differing institutions and areas of special jurisdictions and particular immunities, in which *seigneurs*, priests, village notables and royal officers all had a hand. The confusion was itself the result of the system of unequal privilege, and fostered barriers and divisions by its stress on provincialism. Moreover, the royal authorities were imposed from above and controlled from the central government.

The Assembly aimed to replace this by a more uniform and rational system, embodying equality of treatment and the elective principle. France was divided into eighty-three departments, subdivided into 374 cantons, which were in turn divided into communes. All the 44,000 communes had equal status, similar powers and similar authorities, elected in each commune by the active citizens. This was also the case with cantons and departments, although in these larger units the governing council was elected indirectly in stages.

The reform was not an immediate success.

57

Judicial procedure was reformed in enlightened and humane ways. Arbitrary imprisonment was forbidden. The accused was innocent till proved guilty, trials were to be public and juries were introduced in criminal cases. Barbarous practices and punishments such as torture, branding and breaking on the wheel, were abandoned. The death penalty was retained, though some like Robespierre, argued for its abolition. Even here privilege was abolished. Previously aristocrats had enjoyed the distinction of being beheaded whereas commoners were hanged. In future all would be beheaded. The deputy, Dr. Guillotin, recommended, although he did not invent, the new machine for this purpose, which was named after him.

In their economic legislation the Assembly mainly favoured the progressive, individualist approach and dismantled many of the controls and restrictions of the old regime. They introduced a uniform system of weights and measures. They abolished the system of local tolls and internal customs barriers, although these free trade notions stopped at the national frontier. The guilds and corporations, obstacles to individual enterprise, were suppressed. New types of association, the trade unions, were as unacceptable as the old ones. The Le Chapelier law prohibited associations of workmen.

Reform and the Church

Whatever such measures might do eventually to increase the national wealth, they were of little help with the immediate financial problems. The Assembly had to devise a new tax system to replace the inadequate, unequal one of the old regime. They proposed to do this with three taxes,

the main one falling on all landed property. These taxes were not very productive in the still disordered condition of France, nor would they clear the great debt inherited from former days. There was no question of repudiating this debt. The deputies were financially orthodox, and the middle classes from which they were drawn included many bondholders. Indeed, they had considerably increased the national debt by paying compensation to those whose offices had been abolished.

The solution was to confiscate the vast property of the Church, which the Assembly argued could be seized, since it was not private property and since it was supposed to promote purposes like education which the state would henceforth discharge. The sale of Church property would replenish the Treasury and, pending its sale, the property provided backing for the issue of a paper currency, the *assignats*. As Church land was sold, *assignats* to this value would be called in and destroyed, so that inflation would be avoided.

The move had important consequences. It worked well at first, but in time the temptation to print *assignats* in excess of the resources backing them was too great. The resulting inflation contributed to that economic distress which underlay so much of the popular unrest throughout the revolutionary years. The main purchasers of Church lands seem to have come from the middle classes and the wealthier peasantry. These great beneficiaries became hardened in their resistance to any attempts to put the clock back to 1789 and equally determined to oppose any radical attempts to put it too far forward.

The move also played a part in one of the most fateful acts of the Assembly, its reorganisation of the Church. As the state had commandeered its wealth, the money for the upkeep of the Church would have to come from state funds. Most deputies were soaked in the anti-clericalism of the philosophers, and believed the Church needed a thorough overhaul, the more so if it were to be supported from public money. In the

Civil Constitution of the Clergy in July 1790, the Assembly redrew diocesan and parish boundaries, made bishops and parish priests subject to election and dissolved many of the religious orders. They demanded that all

Top left: in Paris in July 1789 the Third Estate broke the chains that bound it, to the alarm of the nobles and priests. (Bibliothèque Nationale, Paris.) Centre left: in the countryside people groaned under the weight of the tax burden. (Bibliothèque Nationale, Paris.) Bottom left: on the night of 4 August a frightened nobility renounced their privileges. (Bibliothèque Nationale, Paris.) On 12 July blood flowed in the streets of Paris. An excited crowd moved down the rue St. Honoré and hurled itself against royal guards commanded by the Prince of Lambesc, who (above) charged with sabres down. (Musée Carnavalet, Paris.) The crowd dispersed in terror (top centre) in the gardens of the Tuileries. (Bibliothèque Nationale, Paris.)

LA PRISE DE LA BASTILLE.

victoire

prise Du gouverneur

Above: the siege of the Bastille. (Musée de Versailles.) This is at once the best-known and the most misunderstood event in the Revolution. The role of the fortress had been greatly exaggerated by pamphleteers and in fact the governor, De Launay, had only thirty men, a few supplies and seven prisoners. However, the crowd who moved against it were under the mistaken impression that it contained large supplies of arms and ammunition which would serve their cause. The people came from Faubourg Saint-Antoine, and amongst them were sympathetic rebellious soldiery. The drawbridge was lowered but the governor lost his nerve and fired on the rebels (right) (Bibliothèque Nationale, Paris.)
The crowd was now supported by troops of the municipal guard and De Launay surrendered. As he was being taken to the Hôtel de Ville (far right) the mob, unhindered by his escort, slaughtered him. (Bibliothèque Nationale, Paris.)
Bottom centre: a member of the king's household infantry which was disbanded in 1789. (Bibliothèque Nationale, Paris.)

60

Rhine and international agreements, scraps of paper signed by unrepresentative monarchies, should not stand in the way of the rights of the nation. In February the Convention welcomed Brissot's move to declare war on Britain and Holland and in March, on Spain. Soon France was at war with almost all the powers of Europe—'all the tyrants of Europe' as Brissot put it, except Switzerland and Scandinavia.

From early 1793, however, the situation rapidly deteriorated and a new crisis even more alarming than that of the previous summer developed. Dumouriez, far from pressing on to invade Holland, was defeated at Neerwinden. Worse' still, blaming the politicians for his defeat, he tried to march his armies against Paris and, unsuccessful in this, deserted to the enemy along with most of his staff. The Austrian forces pushed over the border on to French territory and behind them came the *émigrés*. Further south, other French armies were forced back from the Rhine. At the same time civil war broke out in France itself. A move by the Convention to raise a levy of 300,000 men met stubborn resistance in some regions, especially in the Vendée. Here the religious measures of 1791 had already created unrest and an attempt to conscript the peasantry brought on an open revolt which local nobles were quick

to exploit. Not surprisingly the rebel armies, having employed to advantage the difficult terrain they knew so well, soon established control of this region.

News of defeat, treason, invasion and counter-revolution poured in on Paris where agitation exacerbated economic distress. Financing the war effort had promoted inflation; the assignat had fallen to about one third of its face value, and food prices had risen sharply from early in the year. Extremist agitators, like the radical priest Jacques Roux, gathered a large following as they voiced popular demands for controls on prices and currency, for requisitioning food supplies and for tough measures against hoarders and speculators. Jacobins as well as the Girondins disapproved of the activity of these *enragés* or wild men. They distrusted their influence over the *sans-culottes*; and disliked their unenlightened programme of economic controls, as well as their petitions, their deputations and demonstrations to put pressure on the assembly, and the violence of their language, which showed little respect for politicians of any kind. But it was the Gironde, still the dominating element in the assembly, and the most outspoken in denouncing both the notion of economic controls and the activities of the *sans-culottes*, who were most

blamed for the Assembly's indifference to the people's demands.

The Girondins became the target of more determined onslaughts as military setbacks added alarm to discontent. They were especially damaged by the defection of Dumouriez since he had been so closely associated with them. They seemed as reluctant to respond to popular demands for drastic measures in this emergency as to those for economic controls. True the Assembly did take steps in March which were to be of great importance. They strengthened

Women played a major role in the Revolution. It was they who brought back the royal family from Versailles. They also played a prominent part in their own clubs. Far left: the three knitters watch the gruesome work of the guillotine. Centre: wealthier women offer gifts to the Convention. Above: Santerre, the brewer of the Faubourg Saint-Antoine, who became commander of the Paris National Guard and was largely responsible for the attack on the Tuileries. He was arrested in 1793 but liberated after the coup d'état *on 9 Thermidor (that is, the eleventh month of the French Revolutionary calendar, in fact 27 July 1794). (Musée Carnavalet, Paris.)*

Above: Louis XVI saying goodbye to his family. (Musée Carnavalet, Paris.)
Centre: the executioner showing the king's head to the crowd. The guillotine was surrounded by 20,000 troops and many people danced about it afterwards, some dipping handkerchiefs in the king's blood. The king's head and body were buried ten feet deep on the same day in the cemetery of Sainte Madeleine near the bodies of his Swiss Guards who were massacred in 1792. (Bibliothèque Nationale, Paris.)
Far right top: medallion of the dauphin as a prisoner in the Temple.
Far right below: the arrest of Chrétien Malesherbes, who at the age of seventy-one had offered to be the king's defence counsel. As a result of his loyalty, was sent to the guillotine. (Musée Carnavalet, Paris.)

the executive by establishing a Committee of Public Safety, set up a Revolutionary Tribunal, and began to reassert central direction by sending deputies out on mission to the localities.

In all this it was the Jacobins who took the initiative, especially Danton. The Girondins aired dislike of a strong executive, the more so since it was being pressed by popular demands and advocated by the Jacobins. The latter openly aligned themselves with the *sans-culottes* and not only intensified their long-standing criticism of the Girondins, but also declared that the Revolution could only be saved with the help of the people. In May, they championed the popular economic demands about which they had been silent before. At the same time the sections denounced the Girondins as hindrances to the determined action

needed to save the Revolution, and demanded that the Assembly should purge these guilty men. By May, three quarters of the sections had submitted such demands and threatened to act themselves if the Convention refused. Another popular revolution was in the making.

Revolution and insurrection

The revolution took place between the 31 May and the 2 June. The Girondins, desperate because of constant criticism, took action which only confirmed popular distrust and hurried on the insurrection. They tried unsuccessfully to have Marat condemned by the Revolutionary Tribunal, set up a Commission to enquire into the recent conduct of the section and arrested popular agitators like Hébert, whom they were later forced to release. The Girondins

also talked of dissolving the Commune, and summoning a new Assembly in the provinces. In short they appealed to their constituencies against Paris, threatening to annihilate the capital if the insurrections continued so that men would 'search the banks of the Seine for signs of the city'.

The effect of all this heightened popular fury and hurried on popular insurrection. At the end of May, delegates from the sections set up a central revolutionary committee which directed operations from 3 May. On 2 June, the Assembly was surrounded by *sans-culottes* and national guards: 'We have come to demand, for the last time, justice on the guilty . . .'. The deputies, prevented even from leaving the Assembly, had to submit to this force and accept a Jacobin motion to expel about thirty of the leading members of the Girondins.

The expulsion of the Gironde, followed as it was by the departure of many alarmed deputies, gave the Jacobins control of the Convention. However, they were in a desperate situation, for the threat of foreign invasion was mounting. The Austrians from the north and the Prussians from the Rhine continued their advances and took three major fortresses in Italy. In the south, Spanish forces crossed the Pyrenean frontier and in the south-east the Piedmontese pushed back in Savoy.

Within France the rebellion of the Vendée was still dominant in the west and seemed likely to move against Paris. To this was now added a widespread outburst of protest from the provinces against the events of 2 June. Over sixty of the eighty-three departments denounced the high-handedness of the Parisians who presumed to interfere

with the elected representatives of the nation.

Important cities like Bordeaux, Lyons, Marseilles and Toulouse went beyond protest, turning out local Jacobins and encouraging armed resistance. This stimulated forces elsewhere, which were hostile to the revolution, to emerge. In Toulon a royalist faction secured control and handed over the port, along with a large part of the French fleet, to the British. In Paris, the popular hero Marat was assassinated in July by the Girondin sympathiser Charlotte Corday. In these circumstances moderates no less than Jacobins felt that only resolute and ruthless action would serve.

At the same time the Jacobins were under constant pressure from below, from the *sans culottes* who had put them in power. The Jacobins had promptly drafted a democratic constitution in June which along with universal suffrage, direct elections and the referendum, recognised society's obligation to provide work for the able-bodied, relief for the needy and education for all. But this, though promising, was not to be immediately implemented.

With the news of defeats and betrayals, with mounting inflation and disrupted food supplies, the popular tension grew. Throughout July and August, the assembly was bombarded with requests from the sections for effective legislation on prices, for stiffer laws against aristocrats and hoarders and for severe punishments against offenders.

The clamour reached a peak early in September with large-scale demonstrations and a mass march on the Assembly. The Jacobins, apart from any special sympathy for a more 'popular' revolution, recognised their crucial importance. These demonstrations represented a danger in that they might, in an excess of furious impatience, sweep away the whole Convention, Jacobins and all; but they also represented, despite their drawbacks, the most zealous forces which the revolution possessed at this desperate time. It was only in order to keep their support that the Convention introduced price controls on food and a wide range of consumer goods, levied a forced loan on the rich, and sanctioned the establishment of 'revolutionary armies' to forage for food. The demonstrators also wanted strict laws against suspects and hoarders of food and revolutionary justice meted out against offenders. Now, under the twin pressures of a national emergency and popular clamour, a new kind of revolutionary government began to take shape and each successive stage was to bring about a new alignment of forces.

The climax of the Revolution

The twelve months from July 1793 to July 1794 saw the Revolution at its most dramatic. Under the rule of Robespierre and the Jacobins it reached its peak of effective government in the Committee of Public Safety, of ruthlessness in the Reign of Terror, and of radicalism in the alliance of Jacobins and *sans-culottes*.

In these circumstances the Jacobin leaders recognised that only the most resolute and ruthless action would be effective. Besides, they had no intention of putting their new democratic constitution into operation; it was for show and for the future, not for immediate use. Its suspension was made official in early October when the Convention decided that the government was to be revolutionary, that is of an emergency character, until the coming of peace.

The main instruments of revolutionary

Far right top: Lepeletier de Saint-Fargeau, a nobleman turned Jacobin, who represented the department of Yonne and who was assassinated by royalists because he voted for the king's death.
Right: Jean-Paul Marat being carried in triumph after his acquittal before the Revolutionary tribunal, April 1793. The Girondins had sought to condemn him for his attacks on those deputies who had tried to save the king's life. (Musée Carnavalet, Paris.)
Above left: a family of sans-culottes (enthusiastic republicans). (Musée Carnavalet, Paris.)
Above centre: an agreement between Royalists and Republicans brought about the pacification of La Vendée after hard fighting. (Bibliothèque Nationale, Paris.)

Revolutionary portraits:
Far left: David's painting of Marat murdered in his bath by Charlotte Corday. (Musée de Versailles.)
Left: Maximilien Robespierre. (Musée Carnavalet, Paris.)
Above: an unknown revolutionary. (Musée de Versailles.)
Below: the chemist Antoine-Laurent Lavoisier who was arrested in 1793.
Below left: sans-culottes *force a passer-by to wear the tricolour cockade. (Musée Carnavalet, Paris.)*

Below: Saint-Just who has become a
favourite of historians because of his youth
(he was a deputy at twenty-five), charm and
good looks and his revolutionary idealism.
But he was cold and aloof, arrogant and
very sure of his power. He was an open
disciple of Robespierre, who was flattered by
his admiration.
Right: his sister Louise. (Musée de
Blérancourt.)

The revolutionary armies were the
achievement of Lazare Carnot, Louis de
Saint-Just, Prieur de la Côte D'Or and
Robert Lindet. They called on volunteers
like those shown here (above right) and
supported the rising generals Jean-Baptiste
Jourdan, Lazare Hoche and Jean Baptiste
Kléber. (Musée Carnavalet, Paris.)
Below left: the forces of the Convention
recapturing Lyons from the royalists.
(Bibliothèque Nationale, Paris.)

government were already in existence from the spring; the executive committees of Public Safety and General Security, and the Revolutionary Tribunals and Committees. What the Jacobins did was to wield them with a new determination and ability. The Convention remained the legislative authority and appointed the main Executive Committee of Public Safety by monthly election. But previous notions of a weak executive and the separation of powers were dismissed for the Jacobins dominated the Convention which, month after month, returned the same twelve Jacobins to the Committee, and debate dwindled.

In earlier regimes the assemblies had been the centres of activity, where the main struggles had been fought out in long verbal battles. Ministers had been shadows. Now that the executive committee was the centre of the real work, the Assembly had to listen to the Convention's explanations and pass the decrees they required. The committee wielded enormous powers over the whole field of domestic and foreign policy, though police matters were left to another body, the Committee of General Security. Earlier ideals of decentralisation likewise were abandoned as the Committee steadily strengthened the central government's grip over all local institutions.

Below: the struggle against foreign rulers was part of the revolutionary cause but it did not prevent bitter internal feuds among the patriots. (Musée Carnavalet, Paris.)

Revolutionary portraits:
Right: the deputy Armonville, nick-named
'Red cap', and a judge of the revolutionary
tribunal.
With the political advance of the sans-
culottes many new forces were at work.
Left: young men at exercise on the
Champs-de-Mars.
Below: a 'republican banquet'.
Below left: a female patriot in patriotically
striped male dress, and her family. (Musée
Carnavalet, Paris.)
Far left, below: a girl in a simple muslin
dress, the new fashion. (Musée
Carnavalet, Paris.)

In December the representatives on mission, hitherto vested with wide powers to eliminate trouble makers, were brought directly under the Committee, their authority limited to that of carrying out the Committee's policies. The local institutions and departments were by-passed, the smaller cantons and communes made the big units. In each of them the central government appointed national agents who were supposed to report to the government every ten days. The Paris commune had its powers restricted. The 'revolutionary' armies of *sans-culottes*, invaluable in the summer, were disbanded, the committees of the sections put under central government, and their leading officials paid or transformed from popular spokesmen to government agents. And along with executive power went ruthlessness. In September 'Terror' became the rule as the processes of revolutionary justice were made more swift and summary and the instruments—revolutionary tribunals and committees—used more fiercely.

The Committee of Public Safety

The direction and the driving force of revolutionary government came from the Committee of Public Safety, the twelve-man team which, with very few changes, ruled France for twelve crucial months. All deputies and Jacobins, they were mainly men of that provincial urban professional middle class which played the major role in all the revolutionary assemblies. Hénault de Sechelles, the chief architect of the Jacobin constitution of 1793, was an exception; he was a former aristocrat and parlementaire. Lazare Carnot, mainly responsible for the organisation of the armies of the revolution, was a former captain of engineers; Claude Prieur de la Côte d'Or, another military engineer, worked closely with Carnot.

Robert Lindet, a lawyer from Normandy, had the special task of supervising supplies and provisions and was assisted by Pierre Louis Prieur de la Morne. Jeanbon Saint-André, a Protestant clergyman and one-time sea captain, concerned himself pri-

marily with reshaping the navy. Bertrand Barère from Toulouse, another lawyer, acted as a kind of public relations man for the Committee, expounding and defending its policies in the Convention. Billaud-Varennes, who had been many things in his time, including a teacher and a pamphleteer, and Collot d'Herbois, actor and playwright, were both extremists with a strong influence in the Commune and the sections. Both were appointed after the extremist agitations of early September, probably to reassure the popular forces and to strengthen the Committee's connections in that important region.

Georges Couthon, a crippled lawyer from

Above: 'each of the same height, that is the true happiness' was the motto of the National Level. (Bibliothèque Nationale, Paris.) The egalitarian spirit was the motivating force of the Parisian sans-culottes *and the Hebértistes.*

the Auvergne, and Antoine Saint-Just, twenty-five years old law graduate, both spent much time on special missions. Couthon, a gentler man than some of his speeches suggested, and Saint-Just, cold and arrogant, were also the close associates and admirers of the dominant figure of the Committee, Maximilien Robespierre.

Robespierre

It was Robespierre, the lawyer from Arras, who came to seem the embodiment of the revolutionary government. He was in his early thirties, a small man, not much over five feet, with a thin, pale face, and a harsh voice. He was always neatly dressed, fastidious in his tastes, and reserved and

On 5 September 1793 Terror became 'the order of the day'.
Below: an execution on the Place de la Révolution, now called the Place de la Concorde.
Marie Antoinette was guillotined on 16 October, followed by twenty-two Girondins, Madame Roland, Philippe Égalité (the former Duke of Orléans) and Madame du Barry. During the Terror some 40,000 people were executed. (Musée Carnavalet, Paris.)
Right: finally there was revulsion against the guillotine. (Bibliothèque Nationale, Paris.)

Above: Philippe Fabre d' Églantine. (Musée de Versailles.)
Below and far right, top: a revolutionary guard. (Musée Carnavalet, Paris.)
Centre: the guillotine.
Far right, top: Marie Antoinette and her children. (Musée de Versailles.)
Far right: the queen on her way to execution. (Bibliothèque Nationale, Paris.)

withdrawn in manner. A bachelor, he lived in modest lodgings, indulged in little social life and had few friends. He was no demagogue and could hardly have looked less like a *sans-culotte*, but he inspired popular trust because of his incorruptibility.

By his adherence to principles and his constant praise of the common man, he had established a reputation as a zealous revolutionary, a formidable parliamentarian and a popular hero. Likewise his criticism of the constitution in 1791, his opposition to Brissot in the Jacobin Club in 1792, and his championship of the Mountain and the popular cause in the Convention, had all kept him prominently in the public eye. Despite this, he had no official supremacy in the Committee, nor was it its dictator. The people in the Committee worked harmoniously as a body and met daily, from early morning till late at night. All those who were in Paris came along and took part in discussions, and if they agreed on the policies, signed the documents. Dissenters abstained. They were determined men, set on saving the republic from counter-revolu-

tion at home and outside enemies, and all were ready and responsible for whatever measures were needed to achieve this end.

It was here, in the Committee and the Convention, that Robespierre had a stronger influence than any other politician. On the Committee he assumed no special 'department' and never went on any mission to visit the armies or the provinces. He was thus constantly on the spot, assiduous in Committee attendance and free to brood over general policies and to make speeches in which he discoursed on the principles and character of the true Republic. He was the Committee's most conspicuous spokesman in the Assembly and the Jacobin club, and his integrity and dedication were never in doubt: 'He will go far', Mirabeau had prophesied, 'he believes what he says'.

The Terror

The new regime showed its resolution in its vigorous onslaughts against the counter-revolutionary forces within France. Its great weapon was terror, the use of fierce intimidation to destroy or deter the repub-

Robespierre proved incapable of giving a lead to those in the Commune and those at the City Hall who supported him. In the early hours of 10 Thermidor, Paul Barras, with 6,000 men, appeared at the City Hall and carried off the Robespierrists as prisoners. Robespierre tried to shoot himself (below left) but succeeded only in breaking his jaw. (Bibliothèque Nationale, Paris.)
Above left: he and twenty-one others were guillotined. (Bibliothèque Nationale, Paris.)
Above: a revolutionary tribunal.
Far left: a revolutionary guard. (Musée Carnavalet, Paris.)

lic's foes and reassure its supporters. Hitherto terrorism had flared sporadically in the shape of lynch law, as in the prison massacres of 1792. From September 1793, when the Convention had decreed that 'terror was the order of the day', it became official government policy. There should be no restraint, said Saint-Just, for 'between the people and its enemies there is only the sword'. In the same month the Law of Suspects decreed the immediate arrest of all persons suspected of disloyalty, a crime it defined in broad and vague terms, and the Revolutionary Tribunal was reorganised to deal more effectively with the increasing number of those accused of treachery.

Under the terror about 40,000 people were executed, and many times that number imprisoned. It was concerned with disloyalty wherever found, not with social class, and the victims came from all walks of life. About ten per cent of them were nobles, six per cent clergy, fifteen per cent middle class, and the great majority poorer classes and peasantry. Some were executed under the economic laws against hoarding and

speculation, but the bulk suffered for broadly political reasons, such as armed rebellions, voting against recruitment, or holding counter-revolutionary opinions. In Paris the guillotine claimed Marie-Antoinette and Madame du Barry, Brissot, Madame Roland and about twenty of the leading Girondins, as well as 'patriots' from earlier days like Barnave, Bailly and the newly named Philippe Égalité, the former Duke of Orléans.

The weight of the new regime also made

Above: the three consuls in the Council of State: Jean de Cambacérès, Napoleon Bonaparte and Charles François Lebrun. (Musée de Versailles.)
With Robespierre gone there was a general relaxation of tension.
Above right: public baths acquired considerable popularity and became fashionable resorts.
Below right: at the Hôtel Richelieu the tone was one of high revelry. (Bibliothèque Nationale, Paris.)

itself felt in those districts which had risen in rebellion. Throughout the autumn Government armies steadily reduced the rebel centres. Marseilles surrendered in August, Bordeaux and Lyons in October, and Toulon was recaptured in December after an artillery bombardment from an 'officer of outstanding merit', the young Napoleon Bonaparte. In the Vendée, insurrection continued to smoulder for years, but the main rebel armies were scattered in October and December by experienced republican troops. Behind the armies came the deputies on mission to punish the rebels. In Lyons the guillotine did not work fast enough for Collot d'Herbois; he called in firing squads to its aid, and then cannon. The victims were herded in batches, mowed down by cannon fire and shovelled into graves. The houses of the wealthy were destroyed and the name of Lyons struck off the map: 'Lyons made war on liberty, Lyons no longer exists'. At Toulon, Barras and Fréron used firing squads for mass executions: 'Every day since our entry, 200 Toulonnais have been shot'. In the Vendée,

Carrier executed Republican vengeance by drowning 2,000 rebels in the Loire, and having another 3,000 shot. Jacobins on the local revolutionary committees throughout France acted as agents, unearthing and denouncing suspects.

Throughout these same months when they were suppressing the internal enemies of the Republic, the Jacobins also had to conduct the war against invading armies on several fronts. Their achievement was astonishing and novel, a great drive to mobilise the nation's manpower and resources for the war effort. 'The Republic', declared the Convention in August, 'is a great city in a state of siege: France must become one vast camp.' It proclaimed a *levée en masse* (mass mobilisation); young men would go to the front, married men see to weapons and food and women make clothing and do hospital work. In fact the first age-groups recruited, eighteen to twenty-five, produced barely half a million recruits.

To feed and equip new forces on this scale, the government had to play a bigger role in directing the economy. Under Lindet, a central food commission saw to the supply and distribution of food according to the needs of the armies and the regions of the country. Under Claude Prieur the munitions industry was directly controlled by the government. State factories were established, buildings commandeered, labour and materials requisitioned. Carnot speedily fashioned a new army and each unit of raw men was seasoned with a few veterans. New tactics were introduced to make the most of their advantages of great numbers and high zeal. New young generals were pro-

moted, and celebrated names made their appearance—Jourdan, Hoche, Pichegru, Bonaparte. By early 1794 France had a million men under arms and a dozen armies in the field. The Austrian advance from the north had been checked at Wattignies, the Spaniards driven back over their frontier, the Piedmontese pushed out of Savoy and the Prussians thrown back across the Rhine.

By the spring of 1794 the national emergency was receding, but the regime became more dictatorial, not less. Terror, instituted as a weapon against the counter-revolutionary enemies of the republic, was now wielded against the revolutionary critics of the government. Prominent among these were the left wing extremists, associated with the popular agitator, Jacques Hébert, who ran a notorious journal, the *Père Duchesne* and was influential in the commune, sections and popular societies of Paris. For the Hébertistes the revolution was still not popular enough. They wanted more measures to ease the social and economic hardships of the *sans-culottes*, and more ruthless repression of those who exploited them. Even though inflation had been checked, prices remained high, wages were never high enough and controls never a complete success. They championed more direct action by the people, more scope for popular bodies to terrorise their enemies, and more power for the people's revolutionary armies.

The Committee's response to this was increasingly cold. The Jacobins were more radical than other middle-class politicians, had more sympathy with the popular movement and were ready to make concessions.

The nobility could now relax again and fashion took on new extravagances. The men sported huge cravats and long canes (above) and even the National Guard assumed a more 'regal' appearance (right). (Musée Carnavalet, Paris.)

They had introduced economic controls, abolished without compensation the remnants of seigneurial rights, made land purchase easier, and furthered schemes for free education. Robespierre and Saint-Just had sponsored a large scheme for distributing the property of suspects among needy patriots, but they would not champion the interests of the *sans-culottes* exclusively, still less allow the control of the revolution to pass into their hands.

The ideals of the Jacobins

The Jacobins' economic ideals were basically different from the *sans-culottes*: they envisaged a free enterprise economy, not one which, like that of the old regime, was choked with controls and restrictions. They were ready to introduce some controls, but these were merely temporary measures to meet the exigencies of a siege economy and the exceptional demands of a wartime emergency. They did not represent, as the *sans-culottes* were reminded, a desire to champion the exclusive interests of a particular class, by the fact that wages and prices were to be contained and labour strictly disciplined. Again the extremist campaigns were alarming and alienating the middle classes, and Jacobism needed to hold the support of these as well as of the *sans-culottes*.

Jacobins preferred to stress the unifying aspects not the divisive ones of class. For them the touchstone was the quality of man's patriotism and republicanism, rather than his occupation or income. They had a suspicion of great wealth and a preference for the modest property-owner, but they did not intend any large redistribution of property for this to them, as to the men of 1789, was an inviolable right. The Jacobins' dislike was directed mostly at the bad Republican rather than at the prosperous property-owner. Moreover, the Jacobins now saw the scene from the point of view of a government. Popular pressure against earlier regimes which the Jacobins had denounced as incompetent, selfish and reactionary was praiseworthy; against their own regime which was effective, enlightened and looked with wisdom to the best interests of all Frenchmen, it was unnecessary and undesirable. Democracy, explained Robespierre, did not mean that all the people in a vast gathering could participate directly in decisions, or that a myriad of small discontented groups could blithely pursue their own fancies regardless of the rest. It meant that they returned delegates to an assembly which made decisions on their behalf; and in practice, the revolutionary government's advance towards ever more centralised control was running quite counter to that more direct democracy in which the *sans-culottes* indulged. The independent activities of the sections, of 'revolutionary armies', and of unofficial terrorism, became objects of disapproval to an authoritarian regime which desired prompt obedience and no rivals. It was ironic; no one had clamoured more loudly for, or done more to help install, an effective government than the *sans-culottes*, but effective government meant a curb on *sans-culotte* freedom.

The Hébertiste movement was all the more unwelcome for adding to its usual activities a new campaign for dechristianisation. The Jacobins generally, it is true, had little regard for traditional religion; they were enlightened rationalists and staunch anti-clericals. The Convention had readily adopted in October 1793 a new Republican calendar, with natural names for the months and a ten-day week: this broke the religious pattern of the year, obliterating Sundays, Saints' days and religious holidays. But unofficially the movement went further. In Paris, promoted by Hébert and the Commune, it spread into attacks on the clergy, compelling them to resign. Churches were plundered, ceremonies prohibited and statues destroyed. Mock processions aped those of the despised religion. The Commune closed down the churches or used them for secular celebrations, with busts of Voltaire and Rousseau replacing the statues of the saints.

The government feared this 'religious terror' would only upset much of their support and give counter-revolutionaries further arguments for discarding the revolution. In November 1793 the Feast of Reason was celebrated in Notre Dame with Reason represented by a woman of the streets, wearing a cap of liberty.

Robespierre in particular disliked it since he believed in God, and insisted that there was an important place in the revolution for religion. He deplored impiety with the strongest epithet a revolutionary could use: 'Atheism is aristocratic!' This was an additional source of confusion at a time when the enemy were moving steadily nearer.

The downfall of Robespierre

To halt the drift towards atheism and social disruption a deistic religion was devised—the cult of the Supreme Being. But there were other dangers, for the Hébertistes by their speculation had emptied the Treasury and weakened the state. Desmoulins in *Le Vieux Cordelier* mounted a counter-attack on them not only for their atheism, but also for their treachery. Moreover, the Committee of Public Safety was now afraid that it would lose power to the Commune and to the Cordeliers Club which the Hébertistes dominated. Danton for his part wanted the machine of Terror dismantled, the end of controls, and a negotiated peace. When in March, therefore, the Hébertistes threatened an insurrection on the model of that of June or September 1793, Robespierre and Danton arranged for their arrest and execution. Six days later Danton, Desmoulins and Hérault went to the guillotine (April 1794) on a charge of conspiracy with foreign financiers. It was an easy action to perform, but it was also significant, for this was the Terror at its height, the summit of Robespierre's dominance. It was to last for just three and a half months.

On 22 Prairial (10 June 1794) Robespierre persuaded the Convention to pass a law which deprived prisoners of the aid of defending counsel and made death the sole punishment. He also sought to control wages in a desperate effort to control the economy. Yet the need for such terror and discipline began to seem more and more unnecessary as foreign armies retreated and France's frontiers seemed secure. In May, Pichegru beat the Austrians, in June, Jourdan routed Coburg at Fleurus, the British fell back into Holland and the Austrians to the Rhine. There was a growing fear of Robespierre and a bitter hatred of his parade of civic virtue and his pride in his own incorruptibility. The cult of the Supreme Being was as unpopular as the cult of Reason, and the great procession in his honour from the Tuileries to the Champ de Mars, organised by the painter David on 8 June, alienated many.

The climax approached when Robespierre recalled many representatives on mission who now began to fear for their lives. However, the real break occurred on 8th Thermidor (26 July 1794) when he rashly spoke in the Convention of defending himself by one last act, namely the removal of a group of enemies whom he did not specify by name. The next day he was shouted down and arrested. He went to the guillotine on 10 Thermidor (28 July); eighty-seven members of the Commune soon followed him.

The Thermidorians

It is wrong to describe the Thermidorian reaction as the end of the Revolution, but it was certainly its climax. Barère and Barras assumed that the government would continue intact for 10 Thermidor was for them but a 'partial commotion'. Within a month, however, the apparatus of the Terror was abandoned; the law of 22nd Prairial was repealed; within six months the regulation of wages and prices was scrapped; within nine months the surviving Girondins returned; within a year Barère himself and his colleagues were on their way

UNITÉ

ET

INDIVISIBILITÉ

DE LA

RÉPUBLIQUE

With the Directory, uniform became necessary for the officials of the state: Far left: a member of the criminal tribunal. Far left centre: a commissioner for war and next to him a general. (Bibliothèque Nationale, Paris.)
The revolutionary tradition continued in the person of Paul Barras (lower left), the ablest man of the Directory, but also lazy, cynical and arrogant. (Bibliothèque Nationale, Paris.) Around him were a court of whom the chief spirits were Mesdames Tallien and Julie Récamier.
Above: in 1796 Talleyrand, former bishop of Autun, returned to Paris from exile. He was to play a major part in French political life. (Bibliothèque Nationale, Paris.)
Centre: emblem of the Republic. (Bibliothèque Nationale, Paris.)

to Devil's Island. The Thermidorians when joined by the released Girondins and a few royalists emerged as a 'republic of proprietors', led by Barras and Fréron, Cambon and Siéyès. They said that they sought a return to 'the principles of 1789'; but swept along by the tide, the Jacobins were hunted down and the Jacobin Club closed. A new terror, but of a different political complexion, had been unleashed. However, press and theatre were free again; and in the salons the style was set by Thérésa Tallien and the widow Josephine Beauharnais. However, as prices rose, so did unemployment, and in March and May 1795, popular insurrections erupted, with demands for the re-enactment of the Law of the Maximum and the 1793 Constitution—'Bread and the Constitution of 1793'. For a moment the 'Furies of the Guillotine' re-appeared. These were ruthlessly suppressed, and in June 1795 the Parisian *sans-culottes* finally ceased to be a major factor in Revolutionary politics. What Generals Pichegru, in April, and Menou in May did to the mob in the *faubourgs* of Paris, General Napoleon Bonaparte with a 'whiff of grapeshot' did to the Parisian Royalists when they rose in October. Significantly the *sans-culottes* did not rise with them, for they were finished politically and the Revolution now became safe for the men of property.

Dominated by the Thermidorians, the Convention completed a new Constitution, the Constitution of the Year III, in August 1795. It was designed for the propertied classes and was largely the work of Boissy D'Anglas. A single-chamber assembly was now seen to be dangerous so the Legislature was now to consist of two houses—a Council of Five Hundred aged thirty or over which was to initiate legislation, and a Council of Ancients numbering 250 who had to be over forty and married, presumably because this made them more responsible, which had the right to veto. Executive authority was vested in five Directors elected by the legislative councils—each holding office for five years. They could neither sit in the Councils nor initiate laws, but they controlled the army and the police, the civil service and foreign affairs. The departments were left as they were, but each was controlled by a commissioner appointed by the Directory—a forerunner of Napoleon's prefect. The deputies were chosen by an elaborate system of indirect election, and property qualifications were needed for the primary and secondary assemblies. And though liberty of speech and of worship were spoken of as sacrosanct, the press was tightly curbed, and political clubs and the right of insurrection were forbidden. The attempt was clear: to create a balanced government in order to prevent the dictatorship of an assembly, a committee or of a single man. Its very rigidity proved to be its undoing.

From Revolution to Empire

In retrospect, the Directory is inevitably seen as an interlude between the Revolution and the inevitable dictatorship. And the post-1799 Bonapartist press destroyed what little was left of its reputation. It saw itself, of course, quite differently, as the end of an ugly road. Although Barras was unscrupulous, immoral and lazy, the rest were men of some worth. Fearing dictatorship, of one man or of a mob, they set up a mixed government. Also, to guarantee continuity and stability and prevent new waves of unrest from left or right, they stipulated that 500 of the 700 legislators must come from the Convention itself. Those who were re-elected were known as 'perpetuals' who saw themselves carrying on the Revolution against royalism, continuing the war, and enforcing the October 1795 decrees against clergy and *émigrés*. Fearing dictatorship, annual elections were prescribed but these only served to guarantee unrest, dissension and disorder.

Far left: members of the Directory in formal attire. (Musée Carnavalet, Paris.) Centre: the Meeting of the Five Hundred ordered by Napoleon Bonaparte was a disaster. He was jeered at and shouted down. (Musée Carnavalet, Paris.) It was the same at the Council of Ancients (above). (Bibliothèque Nationale, Paris.) Only the calmness of his brother Lucien saved the day for him. He summoned his troops who overthrew the Directory bloodlessly.

The new members were moderates who wanted an end to the war and a constitutional government. A few of them were monarchists; many more would have settled for limited constitutional government. Generals Menou and Pichegru made no secret of their royalism.

Economic chaos

The Directory could perhaps have survived this political division. It could not survive the economic chaos and corruption. There was wild inflation because the *mandats*, issued in April 1796 to replace the *assignats*,

Above left: in 1789 the Austrians left
Brussels in a hurry having been alarmed by
the Belgians in revolt who proclaimed the
country the Belgian United Provinces.
(Heeresgeschlichtliches Museum, Vienna.)
Above: the Declaration of Pillnitz, 1791,
showing (from right to left) Frederick
William II of Prussia, the emperor Leopold
and the elector of Saxony, who promised
armed intervention in France, but only if all
the powers would agree. (Kunstbibliothek,
Berlin.) Within a year France was at war
with Austria and Prussia, and volunteers
(left and far left) went to the front to
replace the regulars. The latter had lost
many of their officers, who had become
émigrés. (Musée Carnavalet, Paris.)

103

had soon fallen to one per cent of their face value. The state was internally bankrupt by September 1797, and all classes suffered. The Directory was in part induced to continue the war, not for frontier defence, but in order to draw the treasures of foreign countries into France. Thus Napoleon took 750,000 francs and part of his portrait gallery from the Duke of Modena, 21,000,000 francs from the Kingdom of Naples, and 20,000,000 francs and the promise of more from the pope. Had the war stopped, the French army of a quarter of a million men would have had to be paid from State funds, and these were totally inadequate. It lived on foreign grain and foreign gold.

To financial chaos was added corruption. Many of the supplies Paris required from the provinces never arrived because of smuggling and inefficient administration. Bridges and roads fell into disrepair and the Paris mobs lived on doles. Bids for peace from Britain met a request from Barras for £500,000 before negotiations began; Talleyrand made a similar request in the XYZ affair when John Adams made overtures in 1798.

In this context, the Babeuf conspiracy is understandable. Ever since 1798 'Gracchus' Babeuf had advocated an agrarian law for the common sharing of goods. He was the

first and perhaps the sole French Revolutionary socialist. In the winter of 1795-6 he planned to overthrow the Directory by force, in a conspiracy joined by ex-Jacobins; his plan was based on a series of radiating groups and depended on the rising of the *sans-culottes*. Again, as in 1795, they failed to respond. A police spy reported the plot in May 1796 to Carnot and, as a result, Babeuf and some forty of his associates were either shot or guillotined. The same fate overtook the conspiracy of the royalist Abbé Brottier in January 1797. But Babouvisme was to live on in the writings of his friend, the Tuscan, Philippe Buonarroti.

In the 1797 elections there came an influx of royalists into the Assembly and the great mass of 'perpetuals' was eliminated. Pichegru was elected President of the Five Hundred, and Barbe-Marbois, another royalist, President of the Ancients. Measures were passed favouring priests and the relatives of *émigrés*, but in the Directory, the two proroyalists, Carnot and Barthélemy, were still outnumbered, and the Triumvirate, fearing a royalist coup, appealed to the generals to save the Revolution. Napoleon, who had swept through northern Italy in 1796 and was forcing its treasure back into France had, by the spring of 1797, driven the Austrians north from the Piave and Isonzo, when he responded to the call; so did Hoche

at the head of the Army of the Sambre-et-Meuse. Augereau, Napoleon's lieutenant, marched on Paris; Barthelemy and Pichegru were arrested; the Councils were purged of over 200 deputies, and sixty-five were exiled to the 'dry guillotine' of Guiana. Carnot, the only lucky one, escaped to Switzerland. The date was 18 Fructidor (7 September). It was the first of the coups, and the beginning of the heavy indebtedness to Napoleon.

The rise of Napoleon

From now on, the Directory was dominant over the Legislature and severe measures were taken against priests and returned *émigrés*. In the *coup d'état* of 22 Floreal (11 May 1798) the Directors annulled the elections of their opponents and nominated their own deputies. Blessed by good harvests, the price of grain fell for the first time in a decade. But in fact the Directory, despite a powerless legislature, faced a rising tide of unpopularity, because of religious persecution, the Law of Hostages which provided that relatives of *émigrés* might be seized as hostages, and because of the maritime war with Britain which had forced up prices and kept tariffs high. The Law of Conscription of September 1798 made all unmarried Frenchmen between twenty and twenty-five liable for service but it was bitterly unwelcome and evaded. Added to this the

At first the war went badly for France. Lafayette was far more involved in revolutionary developments in Paris than at the front.
Below: his lieutenant-general, the Marquis de Gouvion-Saint-Cyr, was killed in an attack. (Bibliothèque Nationale, Paris.)
In September General Dumouriez checked the Prussians at Valmy and they evacuated Verdun in October. In November Dumouriez entered Mons (right) and Brussels. (Musée de Versailles.)
In December Prussian troops retook Frankfurt which the Comte de Custine had taken earlier (left). (Historisches Museum, Frankfurt.)

French armies in 1799 met defeat at Stockach, Magnano and Novi.

Meanwhile, fortune favoured Napoleon. In 1797 he had formed the Ligurian Republic (Genoa) and the Cisalpine (Lombardy). At Campo Formio he obtained a guarantee from Austria of the Rhine as the boundary of France, thus securing Belgium, and acquired a bridgehead at Mainz. Venice was given to Austria and in June 1797, a Venetian fleet in French service seized the Ionian Islands and aroused Napoleon's eastern ambitions. With an invasion of Britain a very risky enterprise, and with his power rising dangerously, the Directory resolved to attack Britain through the East and saw the Ionian Islands as a base against Egypt. In May 1798 Bonaparte sailed from Toulon with 35,000 men, took Malta in June and landed at Alexandria in July.

This only further alarmed the Directory and to make matters worse the Belgian Provinces suddenly revolted. In the April 1799 elections, two-thirds of the government candidates were defeated and Siéyès replaced

the senior director, Reubell. Siéyès wanted a new constitution and, with the support of Barras, he carried through a parliamentary coup, offering as justification the defeats on the frontiers and the rallying cry of *la patrie en danger*. The other three directors were persuaded to resign, and the new Director, Ducos, joined Siéyès and gave him the majority he sought. Siéyès was backed by a group who were to prove themselves in a distinct way perpetuals—Murat, Talleyrand and Fouché. Siéyès then looked for a general sympathetic to the cause of the Republic in danger. He approached Joubert, but the latter was killed at Novi. As for Moreau and Bernadotte, they refused. At this juncture—when in fact the tide was turning on the French frontier, since in September Masséna had defeated Suvorov in Italy and the Duke of York was defeated in Holland—Napoleon landed at Fréjus. His campaign in the East had not been a success: he had been blocked by Sir Sidney Smith at Acre, and he had abandoned his troops on the Nile, who now saw him as a

deserter. But his landing and his timing were providential, and he had about him the glamour of victory and a Jacobin past. He was, he liked to say, the child of the Revolution. He was also to be its destroyer.

The Consulate

His plans almost went awry. The legislature was persuaded to meet at Saint-Cloud on the grounds that the Paris mob was unreliable. However, when Napoleon appeared in person, with his grenadiers massed outside, there were many protests about military dictatorship, and such was the poor impression which he made that he was shouted down. It was only his brother Lucien, presiding over the Five Hundred, who saved the day by summoning the troops to drive the legislators from the hall. A remnant of this body declared the Directory abolished and a provisional consulate of Ducos, Siéyès and Napoleon established, until such time as a new Constitution could be drawn up. It was the 18 Brumaire of the Year VIII (9 November, 1799).

But Siéyès had made a mistake. He had expected Napoleon to select his senior officials along Washington's lines and play the role of a president above politics. In fact Bonaparte made himself the First Consul and the power-house of the state. In December 1799 yet another Constitution appeared, the Constitution of the Year VIII. Siéyès and Ducos were persuaded to resign, and were replaced by silent allies in Lebrun and Cambacérès. All three were to hold office for ten years and be re-eligible, but only the First Consul could appoint and dismiss officials and promulgate laws; the second and third had only a 'consultative voice'.

The Council of State was the key to the system. This constituted the group of experts and officials who prepared the laws and ran the government. It was the same with Napoleon as it had been with an earlier *grand monarque*: the Council was the inner bureaucracy, appointed, dependent, ultra-conscientious, loyal and efficient. It appointed prefects and mayors and through

Right: this wooden soldier was used as a signpost to the recruiting office. (Musée Carnavalet, Paris.)
Above top: the Argonne gorge choked with troops after the battle of Valmy. (Musée de Versailles.)
Above: the Austrians were routed by Dumouriez at Jemappes and Belgium was open to invasion. (Bibliothèque Nationale, Paris.)
Left: the battle around Freiburg as French troops threatened Germany. (Historisches Museum, Frankfurt.)

them Paris governed France; local government was bereft of its powers, and died. And in and around the Council were the lieutenants of the Master: Talleyrand, Foreign Minister (1799–1807), Berthier, War Minister (1800–1807) and Fouché, Police Minister (from 1799–1802 and from 1804–1810). No other institution matched the Council. The tribuneship could not initiate measures and was abolished in 1807 and the Legislative Body of 300 members had no powers of debate. It was true that the Senate of eighty members, all over forty and appointed for life, had powers to annul laws, but this power waned, and in the Year XII the Senate was nominated by Napoleon and no

Top: General Jean Baptiste Kléber. (Musée de Versailles.)
Top right: the French defy the Austrians. (Bibliothèque Nationale, Paris.)
Right: the French cross the River Rhine at Dusseldorf. (Musée de Versailles.)
Far right: volunteers leaving for the frontier to the cry of 'Liberty or Death'. (Musée Carnavalet, Paris.)

longer limited in number. In theory there was universal suffrage, but in fact the Senate nominated the members of the assemblies from a 'national list', itself chosen from 'departmental lists' and from communal lists, in an elaborate system of indirect election.

The Press was tightly controlled, and education became a department of state. Even the salons were disciplined and Madame de Stael was banished from Paris. This was absolutism as naked, centralised and thorough as Louis XIV could have wished. He would have found it familiar and acceptable. The prefects were his intendents but more powerful, and they are still there. Napoleon was not only the child of the Revolution, but also the heir to the best in the government of the Bourbons.

The condottiere

There is a curious anomaly about intense nationalism; it is apt to be felt most sharply on the perimeter of the nation. Thus Hitler, the great pan-German, was born across the frontier in Austria; Stalin, who was an autocrat of all the Russias in the line of the Tsars, was born in Georgia; and Napoleon, perhaps the greatest of all Frenchmen, was born French only by accident and raised on the fringes of France.

Perhaps the truest description of him was that he was neither truly a nationalist nor a revolutionary, but he was at heart a *condottiere* of genius, a leader of men. His methods were always more Italian than French, the leanings always Machiavellian. The advice he gave Eugene he followed himself; base your statecraft on dissimulation and strive only to be feared.

Napoleon Bonaparte was thirty on 18th Brumaire. He was born in 1769 in Ajaccio, Corsica, a year after Genoa had sold its stormy island to France. Only a few months before his birth, French troops had crushed the Corsican rebellion led by Pasquale Paoli. Bonaparte was the second son in a

By 1796 Napoleon had achieved considerable distinction.
Top left: the bombardment of Frankfurt by the French on 13 and 14 July 1769. (Historisches Museum, Frankfurt.)
Far left: Napoleon Bonaparte at Arcoli, 1 November 1796. At a critical moment he threw himself into the battle, the flag in his hand. But it was at Rivoli near Lake Garda (left) and at Mantua that the fate of Italy was sealed. (Musée de Versailles.)
Perhaps the main reason for his success was the speed of movement of André Masséna and the 32nd Brigade. In four days, they covered seventy miles and won three battles.
Right: Napoleon Bonaparte by Rouillard. (Musée de Versailles.)

large family of the lesser nobility, and there were four brothers and three sisters, all dominated by their formidable mother, *née* Litizia Ramolino, Madame Mère. His father saw him from the outset as a man of genius: he was lean and pinched in appearance, but with a piercing hawk-like gaze, great will-power and intensity. He went with a scholarship to the military school at Brienne and the École Militaire in Paris, and he went with a purpose; to free Corsica. He studied hard with this intent, and was utterly out of tune with the rich sons of the nobility around him who had come there by easy roads and with no such design. He was commissioned a second lieutenant of artillery in 1785; and he read assiduously, not least Rousseau and the *philosophes*.

Like Caesar before him and like Hitler after, the army was his ladder, his tool and his passion. He wrote a tract or two, but his weapon was the sword, not the pen. He exploited the Revolution and saw it as his cause, and made it at once Corsican and French. In 1792 and 1793 he tried to seize Ajaccio for the revolution, only to be defeated by Paoli, fighting for Corsican independence and prepared to call on monarchists and Anglophils as allies. In 1793 the Bonaparte family was expelled from Corsica, and the France of the Revolution now became his own cause—other, that is, than himself. His batteries helped to expel the British from Toulon in 1793, and his commander, Du Teil, gave him most of the credit. By the age of twenty-four he was a brigadier. With Robespierre's death, he lost his mentor, so he attached himself to Barras, the least reputable of the Directory. Vendémiaire and the 'whiff of grapeshot' brought him the command of the Army of the Interior, the rank of major-general and the hand of Josephine de Beauharnais, one of Barras's discarded mistresses. He may well have loved her for a while, if he had room for any other passions than war. She may have grown in her fashion to love him, for there was an incandescent quality here and immense physical magnetism. However, four days after the marriage, Napoleon was on his way to Italy. The victories of 1796—Lodi, Castiglione and Arcole, and of 1797—Rivoli—to name only the most important of the twenty-six battles won in twelve months, made him a revolutionary hero at a time of economic discontent and political frustration and, in a military sense, were his greatest achievements. He dominated northern Italy as far as Rimini, occupied Florence and Leghorn, compelled the British to evacuate Corsica and merged Milan, Modena and Bologna into the Cisalpine Republic. At Campo Formio the Machiavellian emerged: he gave much of the Venetian Republic to Austria, in return for the Ionian Islands, an advance base for a campaign in the East. To the Corsican, the Venetians, like everyone else, were expendable. And there followed the Egyptian campaign.

In June 1799, as the French were
withdrawing from Syria after the siege of
Acre, the Turks rushed 18,000 men to
Aboukir Bay. On 25 July 1799 Napoleon
Bonaparte, considerably helped by a charge
of Joachim Murat and his cavalry,
overwhelmed the Turks at Alexandria who
were led by Mustapha Pasha (top left).
(Musée de Versailles.) Bonaparte gave the
battle the name of Aboukir to erase the
memory of the earlier battle in Aboukir Bay
(August 1798) when Nelson destroyed his
fleet and cut him off from France.
Above: a British frigate intercepts a French
ship. (Musée de la Marine, Paris.)
When Bonaparte abandoned his army in
Egypt (August 1799) to return to France,
he left Jean-Baptiste Kléber in command.
Kléber had risen fast—a private in 1793, a
general of brigade in 1794. He defeated a
rising of Turks and Mamelukes at
Heliopolis in March 1800, but was
assassinated by a fanatic on 14 June in
Cairo (left). (Musée Carnavalet, Paris.)

113

Bonaparte hoped to win over the leading Muslims in Egypt so he received a delegation of Muslims from Cairo (top). (Bibliothèque Nationale, Paris.)
A year later in August 1799, he left Egypt since victory was impossible and because he believed that the crisis in France warranted his return. In September, Masséna routed the Russians under Korsckoff at Zurich (above) and forced both Suvarov and the archduke Charles to retreat. (Musée des Invalides, Paris.) By the time Bonaparte arrived, French armies were again in complete control of Switzerland, Holland and the left bank of the Rhine.

The man on horseback

Napoleon rendered immense service to France. But the Napoleonic legend, which via Louis and Napoleon became a legacy and via Boulanger, Petain and De Gaulle a heavy liability, is bound up with the autocrat and the adventurer and battles won on foreign soil. The idea of *La gloire* in French history goes back, of course, long before Brumaire, but the first, overwhelming image of Napoleon is of the conqueror.

Originally this was not his intention for, on becoming First Consul, he had offered terms of peace to Britain and to Austria, the surviving members of the Second Coalition, only to have them scorned, for the Austrians were now dominant in North Italy except for Genoa, which they were besieging. Napoleon dispatched Moreau across the Rhine and he drove the army commanded by Kray back to Ulm. He himself crossed the Saint Bernard Pass, entered Milan and struck at Melas's army in the rear. Genoa had already surrendered, its streets piled with corpses from disease and famine. But at Marengo (June 1800) the tide had turned. Helped by Desaix's corps—and by Desaix's own death in action—Napoleon won back North Italy in a single day and the Austrians again abandoned Genoa, Piedmont and Milan. By July, Moreau occupied Minden and in December had won the battle of Hohenlinden; Brune and Macdonald's joint army then moving on Vienna. The emperor was forced to make peace at Lunéville, 9 February 1801. Lunéville destroyed all that was left of the Holy Roman Empire, which Voltaire had said was neither holy, roman nor an empire. Austria ceded to France all territory west of the Rhine, including Belgium, and also recognised the independence of the new republics, the Cisalpine and Ligurian in Italy, the Batavian (Holland) and the Helvetic (Swiss), all of which were formed in the image of France. The Adige became the frontier between France and Austria in North Italy, and Austria accepted the right of France to intervene in Germany in the affairs of the princes. The minor states of Germany were now as much at the mercy of Napoleon as they had been the puppets of Richelieu 160 years before. To save herself, Vienna abandoned Germany; and this too was to be a bitter legacy. The Tsar Paul became the friend of France and revived the Armed Neutrality of Russia, Sweden and Denmark against Britain. In March 1801 Spain ceded Louisiana to France and plans were made for a great Empire in the Caribbean. But the assassination of Paul in March allowed Alexander I to make peace with Britain; and Nelson's victory at Copenhagen destroyed Napoleon's attempt to wreck Britain's trade with the Baltic and the North.

By 1802 Britain had lost almost all her allies. If she had averted a direct French invasion and thwarted Napoleon in Egypt,

France in 1789 showing the boundaries of the gouvernements *or administrative regions, corresponding approximately to the old provinces, into which the country was at that time divided. The Revolution swept away this regional system and created the department, which, under the control of a prefect, became the chief administrative subdivision.*

115

the National Debt had doubled and there was starvation. She controlled the sea but seemed powerless to stop France on land: it was a war of Whale versus Elephant. And so a truce was made at Amiens in March 1802. France had withdrawn from Egypt in 1801; she agreed to restore Malta to the Knights and to evacuate Naples. All of these were but a recognition of facts. Britain surrendered all her own conquests except Trinidad, which had been Spain's, and Ceylon, which had been Holland's. 'A peace which all men are glad of', said Sheridan, 'but no man can be proud of'. It was a triumph as well as a truce for Napoleon, and even if it was short-lived, it was the first time that France had been at peace in a decade. It was the high point of Bonapartism. In August he made himself a Consul for life, in a plebiscite that gave him 3,500,000 votes, to only 8,300 which had the courage to say 'No!' The new constitution gave him the right to choose his successor and to amend the constitution, to make treaties and to dissolve the Assemblies.

Thus fortified he looked west. A French army was sent to Santo Domingo and the negro revolutionary Toussaint l'Ouverture was seized and sent to France and execution. But his followers fought a bloody war against the new Imperialism, and what they failed to do yellow fever abetted for there were over 20,000 French deaths within a year. These facts, and the fear of a revival of war with Britain, led to the abandonment of the dream and the sale of Louisiana to Jefferson's emissaries. Thwarted in the west, Napoleon turned back to Europe. He became, in his own person, president of the Cisalpine Republic and master of Lombardy which was renamed the Italian Republic. He annexed Piedmont, Elba and Parma, and strengthened his French forces in Holland and Italy—all in denial of the terms of Lunéville. In April, he sought to close to British commerce all the ports which he controlled. He published reports that indicated a resumption of the war in the East. Britain protested, and in May 1803 the war was resumed—the war of the 3rd Coalition. More than ever it was the land giant versus the mistress of the seas.

War brought with it the threat of internal sabotage, treason and plot. Napoleon claimed that the Count of Artois alone was maintaining sixty assassins in Paris. In February 1804, the plot of Georges Cadoudal and General Pichegru to murder Napoleon and restore Artois (the later Charles X) was discovered. A month later, the young Duc d'Enghien was kidnapped by French troops on the neutral territory of Baden, brought to Paris and executed on the false charge of having been involved in the Cadoudal-Pichegru plot. And so, in May 1804, and in the interests of the state, Napoleon became emperor. This time 3,500,000 were for and only 2,500 against. On 2 December 1804, the Corsican heir of all the Bourbons took the

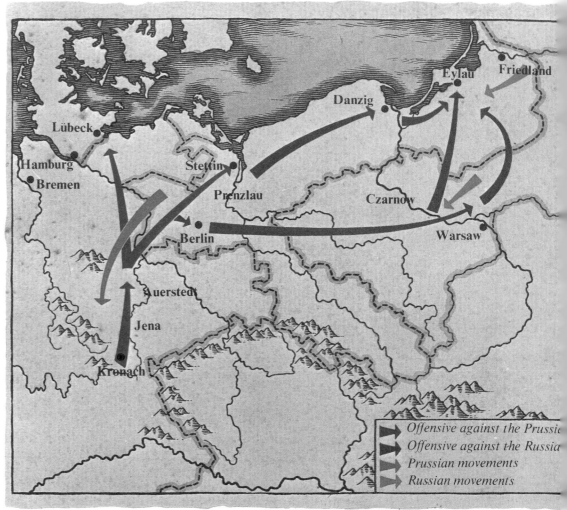

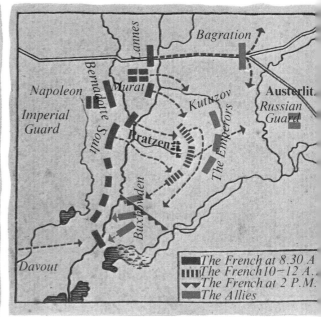

The top map presents a general view of Napoleon's campaigns in central and eastern Europe during 1806–7. After the bloody but inconclusive battle of Eylau in February 1807, when the French met the combined Russian and Prussian armies, Napoleon scored a notable victory over the Russians at Friedland in June 1807, which led to the Treaty of Tilsit.

The smaller map (above right) shows the progress of the battle of Austerlitz (December 1805) in which the French forces defeated the allied Russian and Austrian armies led by Tsar Alexander I and the emperor Francis II. The other map (above left) follows the victorious French campaign in Saxony in 1806 when Napoleon triumphed over one Prussian army at Jena on the same day as Marshal Davout succeeded in defeating another at Auerstedt.

crown of Charlemagne from the hands of Pope Pius VII and put it on his own head. And as David's canvas portrays, a stiff and high ceremonial settled on the parvenu court. The Legion of Honour had been established in May 1802. There were grandiloquent titles, and all the Bonapartes were honoured: Joseph was Grand Elector and Louis Grand Constable—and these were but preludes to even greater honours, for all of Napoleon's brothers, except Lucien, later became kings. Sixteen generals became Marshals of France, and Murat, the ally of Vendémiaire, became Grand Admiral. Napoleon was to create, honour and endow princes and senators: 31 dukes, 388 counts, 1,090 barons and 1,500 knights were created in a great hierarchy designed to make even chivalry and pomp instruments of his statecraft. The Court was to cut Napoleon off in some measure from the nation, but around this particular throne were men of outstanding ability, and of outstanding loyalty and devotion.

The First Consul

But behind the general and the pomp and pageantry of empire lay the achievement: in law, the Church and education.

These were the 'blocks of granite' on which he believed his power rested. In the three years from 1800 to 1803, the Paris years, he carried through most of his reforms. It was as if Louis XIV had been reincarnated with a team of outstanding talent—Talleyrand, Cambacérès, Lebrun, Gaudin, Portalis, and Thibaudeau.

In the codes of law drawn up by his Committees between 1804 and 1810, Napoleon drew heavily on the legislation of the Constituent and Legislative Assemblies. A uniform Civil Code had been a dream since Louis XIV for there were no less than 360 local codes in existence, but until Napoleon all efforts to introduce one had failed. Napoleon himself participated directly in the discussions and his influence and vigour were vital. Indeed, he took greater pride in the Civil Code than in all his forty battles. The Code Napoleon was promulgated in March 1804 and it expressed in law the first principles of the Revolution: equality before the law, including the equal distribution of property amongst sons and daughters, though it was possible to leave a little more to one child if the family contained several children; freedom to work and worship; freedom of conscience, and the secular character of the state. It defined a modern property law freed of all manorial or seigneurial features, and it aimed to make the law uniform, understandable, rational and lucid, in contrast to the customary laws of France and England. In some ways it was strongly conservative for it put marriage and the family (not merely divorce) on a civil basis of the Old Regime. It encouraged firm parental authority both in family and state, for the cohesion of the family group

was itself the basis of the cohesion of the state. The father's control in the family was made absolute; a wife was seen as subject to her husband and could not acquire or sell property without his consent. The principle of divorce was admitted—for adultery, cruelty and for grave criminal offences—but once only.

The Civil Code proved the most durable part of Napoleon's handiwork and it was carried throughout Europe by his armies. In France and beyond, it stood the test of time. It was reinforced by a Code of Civil Procedure, a Commercial Code, which was the least durable of the enactments, and by Criminal and Penal Codes. Yet valuable as they were, the Codes were essentially compromises between the Old Regime and the Revolution, between the authoritarianism of Rome and the liberalism of customary law. Though equality was proclaimed, most of the provisions of the Civil Code, were devoted to the protection of property. In the Criminal Code if penalties were carefully prescribed, they were far from liberal; capital punishment, imprisonment or deportation for life, branding and slavery in the colonies were firmly established; the jury system was tightly curbed and used for judgement, but not for accusation, and the juries themselves were chosen by prefects. While accused persons were tried in public and allowed to speak and to use counsel, they were not allowed to hear the case against themselves as it was being assembled in the preliminary investigation; there was no system of habeas corpus; the Codes were authoritarian in temper and far removed from the spirit of the *philosophes*. They were well designed to detect crime and to ensure fast and speedy trial; but there was no attempt to see the law as a barrier against arbitrary executive power. And in economic terms the Codes said little about wages and conditions of work: it was property, not labour, that was sacrosanct. Employers were given freedom so that the economy should boom and in wage disputes the master's word was taken against the worker's; in the Penal Code, the Le Chapelier Law of 1791 was reintroduced and associations, whether of masters or of workers, were forbidden. Yet, however illiberal they were, the Codes were immensely valuable. In them the permanent shape of the Revolution became clear: the objective was a secular state based firmly on a peasant proprietor class; the protection of private property mattered as much as did equality; but, since all men had equal rights, there was a genuine chance for the 'men of talent' to find their own way to property, fame and fortune.

Napoleon's own taste also emerged clearly: the taste for order and for 'men of talent' not for the common man. Here again he was in the tradition of the Old Regime. Like Louis XIV, Napoleon chose his servants from diverse backgrounds and,

Above: Napoleon in ceremonial robes. He and his family were proclaimed hereditary rulers of France in 1804. The title of king was rejected because of its dangerous associations. Napoleon became emperor instead. (Musée de Versailles.)

as Louis had been frightened by the Fronde, so Napoleon had seen enough of the *sans-culottes* and of the extravagances of the Directory to judge them harshly. Also, much in the same way as Jefferson, the democracy he sought was that in which able men would rise rapidly to the top. It was to be equality to allow the flourishing of unequal talents of unequal men. And what the Codes did in law, Fouché did in practice at the Ministry of Police: it was a regime that offered a widening of opportunity, and also an extension of censorship and repression. By 1810 each department had a single newspaper, tightly controlled by the prefects and by 1811 all the Paris newspapers had been confiscated.

The same spirit permeated the educational system. Primary education remained in local hands and was seriously handicapped by lack of funds. The secondary schools of the Directory were replaced by *lycées*, advanced secondary schools in which military drill and style were curiously married to a classical curriculum. By 1814 this had become and was to remain one of his great achievements. But it was, of course, masculine. As he wrote in 1807, 'What we ask of education is not that girls should think, but that they should believe'.

In 1808 an Imperial University was set up, the Grand Master of which was the educational autocrat of the whole system. A degree from the Imperial University became a prerequisite for teaching. There was even for a time an Imperial Catechism, to teach loyalty to the Emperor. Napoleon also gave new life to those creations of the Convention which were its most valuable legacy: the École Polytechnique, set up in 1795 to train engineers, the École Normale Supérieure, to train teachers, and the Institut de France. Much was done to encourage industry and applied science with technical schools, rewards for invention and industrial exhibitions. But again the intention was clear—education was a department of state, and its watchwords were training, discipline and centralisation. Some of its discipline lasted a very long time.

Central to the Napoleonic strategy was good relations with the Church. If he could secure this he would, at one blow, weaken both royalists and revolutionaries, and gain the support of the great number of faithful

Left: this famous painting by David shows the crowning of Napoleon in the cathedral of Notre Dame on 2 December 1804. Pope Pius VII came to Paris and invested Napoleon with the sword and sceptre of empire and was proceeding to crown him when Napoleon took the crown from the pope's hands and crowned himself. Napoleon then put a second crown on the head of the empress Josephine. (Musée de Versailles.)

Catholics. The clergy, he said, would join the police in generating contentment. To him, the arch secularist, religion was necessary, not for its own sake but for his, as a further buttress to loyalty and sentiment. 'In religion', he said, 'I do not see the mystery of the Incarnation, but the mystery of the social order'. 'If I were governing the Jews, I would restore the Temple of Solomon'.

The Concordat concluded with the pope in 1801 and sanctioned in 1802 was, again, primarily his own handiwork. All bishops were required to resign their sees and the bishoprics were regrouped so that there were now ten archbishoprics and fifty bishoprics. Napoleon nominated them and they were consecrated by the pope. The clergy took an oath of obedience to the

Government and got in return, as good servants of emperor as well as God, a fixed salary. The bishops were given absolute authority over them but ecclesiastical property, confiscated in the heyday of the Revolution, and, bought by the *bourgeoisie* and the peasants still remained in the hands of its purchasers. Roman Catholicism was recognised as the 'religion of the great majority' of Frenchmen, but equal rights were granted to other faiths—a basic principle of the secular state which was unknown anywhere before the Revolution. In other words, the spirit like the mind was disciplined in his service and the Church, like the schools, became a Department of State. The *Journal des Curés*, the only clerical newspaper to appear after 1806,

carried his imprimatur, sermons were strictly censored and there were to be no papal bulls, papal legates or investigations from Rome. But if it was to gain little for Pius VII, at least most of the religious orders returned, as did the Sabbath and the Gregorian calendar. Also the Concordat ended Gallicanism.

Yet when the quarrel with Rome came it was not over these issues. The strongly Gallican spirit in France long pre-dated Napoleon; his attempts to exploit it for his own purposes had the effect of driving his clerical opponents into ultramontanism, that is they recognised the pope as the supreme head of the Church. Pius VII disliked the extension of the Code Napoleon to Italy, since it authorised divorce; Napoleon despoiled Rome of the Legations of

Bologna and Ferrara, which he added to the Kingdom of Italy, and he handed over Ponte Corvo and Benevento to Bernadotte and Talleyrand respectively. Pius objected to Joseph Bonaparte's accession to the throne of Naples, and in 1806 he refused to expel the enemies of France from the Papal states. In May 1809 Rome was annexed by France; in June Pius excommunicated Napoleon and the pope was arrested in the following month and imprisoned in Fontainebleau.

In the end the pope returned to Rome as a result of the allies' triumph at Leipzig, and his steady resistance undermined all Napoleon's efforts. Napoleon found that it was his own unbridled ambition and not the Concordat which succeeded in alienating

many Catholics for he tied Church and state so closely together that their alliance has been a continuous source of tension and danger to France. However, the Concordat survived the quarrel and remained in force until 1905.

Law, Church and education were, then, the instruments of this enlightened despot and far more successful and durable than those of his eighteenth-century precursors, mainly because of his own abilities and his organising and technical efficiency. However it is only fair to add that the success of Napoleon's reforms was due not only to his own talents, but also to the fact that the Revolution had swept away all the interests, privileges, habits and established groups whose opposition had blocked similar

Far left: Napoleon's favourite writer, Chateaubriand, an émigré noble who returned to France in 1800 and served under Napoleon as minister to the Republic of the Valais; he resigned after the execution of the Duc d' Enghien in 1804 and went into exile again. He supported the Bourbon restoration and served as ambassador to Britain in 1822. His works marked the beginning of the French romantic movement. (Bibliothèque Nationale, Paris.)
Above: Chateaubriand's friend Madame Récamier (painted by David) whose salon was a centre of society and gossip. (Musée du Louvre, Paris.)
Centre and top: salons and cafés flourished, even if Napoleonic court life was stiff and formal. (Bibliothèque Nationale, Paris.)

changes since the time of Louis XIV. Absolutism ensured order and it came close to guaranteeing prosperity.

In 1800 the Bank of France was established with the sole right of issuing banknotes. There was active state interference in industry, laws to regulate the supply of food and for the registration of workers with the police. The wars with Britain were calamitous to trade, but a stimulus to industry. The wool and silk trades prospered; the Government paid its bills promptly, helped by foreign treasure brought in by Napoleon's armies; the French peasant who in 1789 kept only nineteen out of every 100 francs he earned kept seventy-nine after 1800. Indeed, the regime was based on the support of two classes, the workmen, whom Napoleon feared and who gave him an illogical devotion, and the peasantry. The last were the great beneficiaries of the Revolution who, having profited from it rejoiced now to see its excesses curbed. By 1810 there were seven million rural proprietors in France which was all but self-sufficient as its agriculture flourished. It

was of course, after Russia, the most populous state in Europe: some 26,000,000 against divided Italy's 17,000,000, Britain's 15,000,000 and Spain's 11,000,000. France's armies had battle experience and, at least until the Russian campaign of 1812, almost unlimited numbers. The army poised to cross the Channel in 1805, had 200,000 men of whom more than half had war experience. This was a strong, cohesive and disciplined state. In the years of the Consulate, Napoleon gave it the stamp of his own authority and energy, his realism and detail, his respect for order and his scorn for abstract rights. The student of Rousseau had moved a long way in a decade. So had the Revolution.

The Empire to Tilsit

The years of the Consulate revealed a ruler of outstanding ability who had turned from war to peace. However, after the collapse of the Treaty of Amiens, the old image was restored, Napoleon as Attila the destroyer. The state he commanded was so strong and the cause he was thought to champion so explosive and popular, that

for a decade he swept through Europe as the Goths had done twelve centuries earlier. As a result, the war of the Third Coalition was total war of a kind that was unknown before.

It began with the attempt to invade Britain. Nelson's blockade of Villeneuve's fleet at Toulon and Collingwood's blockade of Ganteaume's fleet at Brest prevented the assembling of the transports: Villeneuve escaped to the West Indies and returned to be checked at Finisterre. He put in to Cadiz to refit and Nelson, prowling the Atlantic in baffled pursuit, was able to overtake him at Trafalgar, in October 1805, and by his victory, end the risk of invasion and give Britain supremacy at sea which was to last for a century. It was only these ships which stood between Napoleon and possible world dominion. In the meantime Pitt had created a Third Coalition of Britain, Alexander of Russia, Austria, Sweden, Sicily and Naples, whilst Prussia equivocated.

To meet the Austrian danger Napoleon broke up the armed camp and the 200,000 veterans of the Army of England were

dispatched East in seven divisions under the ablest commanders in modern history: Ney, Marmont, Davoust, Augereau, Soult, Lannes and Bernadotte. With them went Murat with the cavalry and Bessières with the Imperial Guard of 10,000 men. They covered 200 miles in a fortnight, faster than Austria or Russia believed possible and before either of them had time to plan their defence. As a result Mack was surrounded, overwhelmed and surrendered with 25,000 men at Ulm in October. The following month Napoleon entered Vienna.

Napoleon called up about 1,500,000 *men. The grenadiers were his elite corps and were devoted to him. This picture (above left) by David shows the emperor giving the imperial eagles to each regiment the day after his own coronation. (Musée de Versailles.)*
Above: an officer of the 5th hussars.
Far left: an officer wearing his bearskin with a red plume and a badge of the imperial eagle. (Bibliothèque Nationale, Paris.)

then west of the Vistula. Frederick William III fell back into East Prussia hoping for Russian help. By December 1806, Napoleon was in Warsaw.

At last Russia moved again. Eylau (February 1807) was a drawn battle with heavy losses on both sides. And though each member of the Coalition talked of action, no common action was taken. At Friedland in June the Russians were overwhelmed and driven across the River Nieman. The two rulers, the emperor and the tsar, met in July 1807 on a raft moored in the river and signed the Treaty of Tilsit.

Tilsit was the climax in the Napoleonic story: the high point of empire. The two emperors divided Europe between them. Napoleon dominated the West, from the Nieman to the Channel. Prussia was heavily despoiled when her Polish acquisitions became a Grand Duchy of Warsaw which Napoleon gave to the King of Saxony; her lands west of the Elbe went to form a new Kingdom of Westphalia, given to Napoleon's brother Jerome; her army was to be limited in size and she was to close her ports to British trade. Alexander for his part recognised France's acquisitions and ceded the Ionian Islands; he was urged to take Moldavia Wallachia from the Ottoman Empire and was promised French help in the attempt. After the destruction of the Holy Roman Empire, the Ottoman was to suffer in a similar manner. Thus both rulers agreed to fasten the shackles of the Continental System on Europe, to keep British and neutral shipping from trading with Europe and to isolate, blockade and finally to destroy Britain. Tilsit was the Napoleonic system at its zenith. Everything hereafter was to be anti-climax.

Napoleon now found that his lines of communication were extended and therefore the Allies, not least an impetuous Tsar, resolved to attack. The result of this was that Napoleon won what was probably his greatest victory—Austerlitz, north of Vienna, on the anniversary of his coronation. His losses were 9,000 out of 70,000; the Austrians and Russians lost 30,000 out of 80,000. Partly it was speed of movement; partly great tactical skill; most of all brilliant leadership with plans communicated frankly to all his men in advance. 'It is by speaking to the soul that men are electrified'. Austria made peace and Russia hurriedly withdrew into its own territory. Ferdinand pulled back to Sicily, safely sheltered by the British fleet and, in January 1806 Pitt died, broken by thirteen years of war. By the Treaty of Pressburg Austria surrendered all her Italian possessions—some of them the ancestral estates of the Habsburgs. The Holy Roman Empire was formally abolished.

Napoleon now organised an array of satellite states: his brother Joseph was made King of Naples and Louis, King of Holland. The Confederation of the Rhine was set up as a pro-French barrier in Europe and it made a defensive alliance with France; 63,000 Rhinelanders fought in French armies.

Prussia at last decided to move, only to be destroyed at Jena and Auerstedt in October 1806. Napoleon then marched through Berlin, from which city he issued the Berlin Decrees enforcing the Continental System and a blockade of Britain by the whole of Europe. He demanded the surrender of all Prussian territory, first west of the Elbe,

Above: Napoleon and Queen Louise of Prussia at Tilsit where, despite her tears and protestations, Prussia was humiliated. (Museum für deutsche Geschichte, East Berlin.)
Below: the display of the grenadiers of the Grand Army given as hospitality for the Russians. (Bibliothèque Nationale, Paris.)

Chronological Charts

THE OVERTHROW OF THE MONARCHY IN FRANCE

	Internal history	Foreign policy	Events in Europe
1789	Meeting of the Estates-General (5 May) Oath of the Tennis Court (20 June) Storming of the Bastille (14 July) Abolition of privileges (3–4 August) Declaration of the Rights of Man (26 August)		Act of Union in Sweden Revolt of Austrian Netherlands Establishment of Belgian Republic
1790	Civil Constitution of the Clergy Priests required to swear allegiance to the Civil Constitution	Repudiation of the Family Compact	Austrian forces overthrow Belgian Republic Pope condemns Civil Constitution of Clergy End of Russo-Swedish War Accession of Leopold II of Austria
1791	Flight of the king Constitution approved by Constituent Assembly and ratified by the king Legislative Assembly meets	Ultimatum to the Elector of Trier Avignon annexed to France	Austria and Turkey sign treaty of peace Declaration of Pillnitz Turkey defeated by Russia
1792	Storming of the Tuileries (10 August) September Massacres (2–5 September) First session of the Convention (20 September) Abolition of the monarchy (21 September) Trial of the king (11 December)	War with Austria (20 April) The Brunswick Manifesto (25 July) Battle of Valmy (20 September) Battle of Jémappes (6 November) Conquest of Belgium	Treaty of Berlin between Austria and Prussia Accession of Francis II of Austria Assassination of Gustavus III of Sweden End of Russo-Turkish War
1793	Execution of the king (21 January) Rising in La Vendée Committee of Public Safety Constitution of the Year I	Annexation of Nice (31 January) War with Britain (1 February) Battle of Wattignies (16 October) Bonaparte recaptures Toulon from British (19 December)	Formation of First Coalition against France Meeting of Polish Diet Second Partition of Poland

FRANCE FROM ROBESPIERRE TO THE EMPIRE

	Internal history	Foreign policy	Events in Europe
1794	Fall of the Dantonists Cult of the Supreme Being Fall of Robespierre	Invasion of Catalonia Capture of Antwerp and Cologne Invasion of Holland	Habeas Corpus Act suspended in Britain Polish revolt crushed British capture Corsica
1795	Attempted insurrection of Prairial White Terror Formation of the Directory	Treaties with Prussia, Holland and Spain Batavian Republic formed under French protection	Acquittal of Warren Hastings Failure of Quiberon Bay expedition
1796	Suppression of *assignats* Babeuf conspiracy	Bonaparte's Italian campaign Moreau's campaign in Germany	Failure of attempted French invasion of Ireland Corsica returned to France
1797	Royalists triumph in elections *Coup d'état* of 18 Fructidor	Battles of Rivoli and Mantua Establishment of Cisalpine Republic Treaty of Campo Formio	Accession of Frederick William III of Prussia Mutinies in the British Navy
1798	Electoral success of the Jacobins *Coup d'état* of 22 Floréal	Campaign in Egypt	Rebellion in Ireland suppressed Nelson's victory at Aboukir Bay
1799	Return of Bonaparte *Coup d'état* of 18 Brumaire The Consulate and the Constitution of the Year VIII	French repulsed in Syria Overthrow of Cisalpine, Roman and Helvetic Republics	Combination laws prohibit trade unionism in Britain Second Coalition against France
1800	Constitution approved by Plebiscite Attempted assassination of Bonaparte	Austrians defeated at Marengo and Hohenlinden	Act of Union between Britain and Ireland
1801	Measures against the Jacobins Concordat re-establishes Roman Catholic Church in France	Peace of Lunéville Treaty with Russia	British naval victory at Copenhagen Paul I of Russia murdered
1802	Amnesty for the *émigrés* Bonaparte consul for life Constitution of the Year X	Peace of Amiens Peace with Turkey Annexation of Piedmont	
1803	Laws restricting workers' freedom Cadoudal and Pichegru conspiracy	Intervention in civil war in Switzerland Army encamped at Boulogne for invasion of England	Britain at war with France
1804	Execution of the Duke of Enghien Napoleon crowned emperor	France and Russia break off diplomatic relations	William Pitt British prime- minister
1805	Napoleon becomes king of Italy	Russians and Austrians defeated at Austerlitz	British victory over French and Spanish fleets at Trafalgar
1806	Napoleon's breach with the pope	End of the Holy Roman Empire Prussians defeated at Jena and Auerstedt Berlin Decrees	Death of William Pitt
1807	Disgrace of Talleyrand	Battles of Eylau and Friedland Treaty of Tilsit	British fleet bombards Copenhagen

Further Reading List

The American Revolution
M. Beloff (ed.), *The Debate on the American Revolution* (London, 1960)

L. H. Gipson, *The Coming of the Revolution 1763–1775* (London, 1954)

J. C. Miller, *Origins of the American Revolution*, rev. ed. (California, 1959); *The Federalist Era 1789–1801* (London, 1960)

C. L. Becker, *The Declaration of Independence* (New York, 1942)

Esmond Wright, *Washington and the American Revolution* (London, 1957); *Fabric of Freedom 1763–1800* (London, 1965)

C. S. Sydnor, *American Revolutionaries in the Making* (New York, 1965)

E. S. Morgan, *The Birth of the Republic 1763–89* (Chicago, 1956)

L. D. White, *The Federalists* (New York, 1948)

The French Revolution
A. Cobban (ed.), *The Debate on the French Revolution* (London, 1960)

G. Lefebvre, *The Coming of the French Revolution*, Eng. trans. by R. R. Palmer (London, 1968)

R. R. Palmer, *The Age of the Democratic Revolution*: Vol. I *The Challenge*; Vol. II *The Struggle* (Princeton, 1959–64); *Twelve who ruled* (London, 1959)

G. Rudé, *The Crowd in the French Revolution* (London, 1959)

A. Goodwin, *The French Revolution* (London, 1959)

J. M. Thompson, *The French Revolution*, rev. ed. (Oxford, 1955); *Robespierre* (Oxford, 1939); *Napoleon: his rise and fall* (Oxford, 1952)

Acknowledgments

9 United States Information Services; 12 Centre right, U.S.I.S.; 14 Below, Muller; 16 Muller; 17 U.S.I.S.; 19 Below right, U.S.I.S.; 20, 21 Mansell Collection; 22 Muller; 23 Below, Muller; 24, 25, 26 Mansell Collection; 27 Above, Josse. Below, U.S.I.S.; 28 Muller; 29 Left and centre, Muller. Right, Josse; 30, 31 Muller; 32 Above, Muller. Below, Josse; 33 Muller; 34 Josse; 34–35 Muller; 36 Muller; 36–37 Above, Muller; 37 Josse; 38 Above, Muller; 40 Muller; 46, 46–47 Muller; 48, 48–49, 49 Josse; 52–53 Josse; 55 Josse; 56 Josse; 58–59 Josse; 60 Above, Josse; 62 Left, Josse; 63 Josse; 64 Centre, Abeille; 64–65 Josse; 65 Above, Josse; 68 Josse; 70 Centre, Josse; 72, 72–73, 73, 74–75, 76, 76–77, 78 Josse; 79 Below, Josse; 80, 81, 82, 82–83 Josse; 83 Below, Josse; 84 Left and right, Muller; 85, Josse; 86, 86–87, 87 Josse; 89 Below, Josse; 90 Josse; 91 Above centre, Josse; 92 Below left, Josse; 92–93, 94, 95, 96–97, 97 Josse; 99 Right, Josse; 100, 100–101, 102, 102–103 Josse; 105 Above, Josse; 106 Josse; 107 Above and right, Josse; 108 Above left and below, Josse; 109, 110, 111, 112–113, 113 Josse; 114 Below, Josse; 117, 118–119 Josse; 121 Centre, Josse; 122–123 Josse; 124 Above, Josse.

Index